How to Become an Exceptional DBA

2nd Edition

by Brad M McGehee

First published 2008 by Simple-Talk Publishing

Cambridge, UK

Copyright Brad M McGehee 2009

ISBN 978-1-906434-23-6

The right of Brad M McGehee to be identified as the author of this work has been asserted by him in accordance with the Copyright, Designs and Patents Act 1988.

All rights reserved. No part of this publication may be reproduced, stored or introduced into a retrieval system, or transmitted, in any form, or by any means (electronic, mechanical, photocopying, recording or otherwise) without the prior written consent of the publisher. Any person who does any unauthorized act in relation to this publication may be liable to criminal prosecution and civil claims for damages.

This book should not, by way of trade or otherwise, be lent, sold, hired out, or otherwise circulated without the publisher's prior consent in any form other than that in which it is published and without a similar condition including this condition being imposed on the subsequent publisher.

Editor - Tony Davis

Contents

Introduction .... **vii**
    What this Book Covers x
    Your Feedback x

Chapter 1: Why Should I Become an Exceptional DBA? **13**
    What is an Exceptional DBA? 13
    An Exceptional DBA is in the Top 10% of Their Profession 15
    Why Bother? 15

Chapter 2: Characteristics of the Exceptional DBA **19**
    Embraces Change 23
    Enjoys Learning 23
    Accepts Responsibility 24
    Maintains Professionalism 24
    Trustworthy 25
    Dependable 26
    Hard-Working 26
    Can Work Well Independently or in a Team 27
    Manages Time Well 28
    Can Communicate Effectively, Both Orally and Verbally 29
    Listens Well 30
    Realistic 31
    Flexible 32
    Patient 33
    Persistent 33

    Enthusiastic 34

    Self-Confident 34

    Thinks Before Acting 34

    Mature 35

    Summary: Assess your Strengths and Weaknesses 36

Chapter 3: Specialize (You can't do it all) 37

    What exactly is a DBA? 37

    An A-to-Z List of Typical DBA Tasks 38

    Choosing a Specialty 47

    Summary: Specialize but be Adaptable 50

Chapter 4: Hone Your Skill Set 51

    Where Does Formal Education Fit In? 51

    Mastering DBA Technical Skills 57

    How to Obtain DBA Technical Skills 59

    Self-Study Booking Learning 61

    Mastering DBA Soft Skills 62

    Summary: Starting Honing Your Skills Today (and don't stop). 66

Chapter 5: Is Professional Certification Necessary? 67

    SQL Server Certification 68

    Benefits of Certification 73

    Should I Get Certified as a DBA? 76

    Summary: There is Little Downside to Certification 78

Chapter 6: Participate in the SQL Server Community 81

    Benefits of Sharing Your SQL Server Knowledge 81

    How Can I Contribute to the SQL Server Community? 85

Summary: Participate in the SQL Server Community Today.... 96

Chapter 7: Manage Your Career, Don't Let It Manage You....97

Define a Career Path.. 97
Create a Plan and Set Goals.. 101
Establish New Goals on a Yearly Basis.................................... 103
Take Action to Attain Your Goals.. 103
Revaluate Goals and Long-Term Career Plans as Needed 104
Summary: It Takes a Conscious Decision on Your Part 105

Chapter 8: Manage Your Brand Within Your Organization .107

Developing Your Brand 108
Summary: You Can't Be All Things to All People................... 119

Chapter 9: Manage Your Online Brand..121

What does it mean to "Manage" your Online Brand? 121
Step 1: Discovering your Online Brand 123
Step 2: Managing your Online Brand....................................... 125
Step 3: Expanding your Online Brand...................................... 125
DBAs and Social Networking Websites 128
Projecting a Professional Image on the Internet: Dos and Don'ts.. 130
Summary: Start Managing your Online Brand Today 132

Chapter 10: Get An Exceptional DBA Job 133

The Job Search 138
Applying for the Job... 144
How to Make a Good First Impression in Your New Job........ 153
Summary: Getting an Exceptional DBA Job is Hard, but the Rewards are High 154

v

Chapter 11: The Exceptional DBA's Code of Conduct 155

What is a Code of Conduct? 155

How Can a Code of Conduct be Useful to DBAs? 156

How Should a Code of Conduct be Implemented and Enforced? 157

The Exceptional DBA's Code of Conduct 158

Summary: Exceptional DBAs are defined by their Actions 163

Chapter 12: Best Practices for Becoming an Exceptional DBA 165

Best Practices 165

Summary: The GOYA Principle 171

INTRODUCTION

I have worked with database applications for most of my career, and have been a SQL Server DBA for the last thirteen years. I started with the computer industry in 1981, the year the first IBM Personal Computer, running DOS 1.0, was released. In fact, I owned one of the first models off the production line.

My first exposure to a database application was in 1982. It was called TIM (Total Information Management) and was written by some guys in Lenexa, KS, in ROM BASIC, the version of BASIC that was built into the first IBM PCs. TIM was slow, hard to use, and very buggy, but it whetted my taste for databases. In 1984, the same developers built a product suite called Smartware, which included a more-sophisticated database application. This is when I first learned how to design databases and develop database applications.

It wasn't until 1996 that I began to get serious about being a full-time DBA. At the time, I was working as a Microsoft Certified Trainer, teaching virtually every certification class Microsoft offered at the time, including networking, development, Exchange, and SQL Server. I soon realized that I could not keep up with that much technology and that I needed to specialize. I considered many options, finally narrowing it down to becoming a DBA, specializing in Microsoft SQL Server. One of the deciding factors was my positive past experience working with databases.

I quit my job as a trainer and set out to become a DBA. While I had some experience with databases, and a good technical knowledge of SQL Server (from teaching it), I had never worked with databases on a full-time basis. Lacking this "real" experience, I knew I was taking a risk, but you have to start somewhere.

I got my first full-time DBA job with a company that had many full-time DBAs on staff. Unfortunately, none of the other DBAs wanted to share their knowledge with me. I was the new kid on the block and they wanted to see me sink or swim on my own. While I was familiar with the technical aspects of using databases such as SQL Server, my lack of day-to-day practical DBA experience was making life tough. It was hard to admit at the time, but I really didn't know what DBAs did day in and day out. I went through a painful year,

Introduction

learning most everything the hard way, making many mistakes and learning from them. On the other hand, I was starting to get discouraged working for this company.

Then opportunity knocked. While casually browsing the Internet one day during lunch, I found a SQL Server DBA job offered at another company. On a whim, I e-mailed my resume, and within a few hours, a recruiter called me, wanting to know if I could attend a job interview the following Monday. Things were happening a little fast all of a sudden.

I went to the job interview and was hired on the spot. I was a little surprised at how fast I was hired, and it was a big boost to my confidence. I started the new job within two weeks. Then I got a new surprise. This DBA position was a brand new position and I had to handle all of the DBA work myself. There was nobody to ask for help or for guidance. I was on my own. I guess I should have asked more questions during the interview. I had learned a lot from my previous experience, but my confidence in my skills was still low.

So there I was, in a new job, and the company was dependent on me to be their first, full-time SQL Server DBA. I have to admit, it was a little unsettling. However, I guess the situation motivated me to very quickly rise to the occasion. I immediately immersed myself in every piece of information I could find on how to be a great DBA. I read books, I searched the Internet, I attended conferences, spoke with other DBAs, and I worked very hard. Very quickly, my self-confidence in my skills went up. My skills were noticed and appreciated by my manager. Once I got on this path of trying to excel in my job, I found I couldn't stop. The company had put a lot of faith in me, and I didn't want to disappoint them.

As I progressed, I wrote down almost everything I learned so that I wouldn't forget it. Eventually, I had a huge document on my hands, and it was starting to become hard for me to find information when I needed to refer back to it later. To remedy this problem, I decided to convert the document to HTML and use a desktop search engine to find the information I needed. Soon after starting this project, I realized that, for about the same amount of work, I could create a simple website and share the information I had collected with others. I figured that if I could use this information, then perhaps others might also. And was I ever surprised. Once I launched the website, SQL-Server-Performance.com, it immediately became popular. I did not realize that there were that were so many DBAs seeking the same kind of information I was seeking. With the positive reception of the website, I was motivated to

Introduction

continue to add new content, which forced me to continue to learn even more so that I could share what I learned.

As the website became established, I began to get e-mails from people wanting to learn how to become a DBA. The same types of questions also appeared in the forums of the website. At the time, I answered these questions the best I could. I even wrote an article called "The Self-Taught DBA", which received a lot of attention. However, I never addressed the question of how someone becomes a great DBA.

Eventually, I began speaking at SQL Server conferences and started meeting lots of DBAs, novices and experts alike. I observed that most DBAs fell into one of three groups. One group of DBAs fell into their job by some career accident and it was just a job to them. Another group of DBAs were at the novice or intermediate level and really wanted to become expert DBAs and take their career seriously. The final group comprised career DBAs who had become experts through lots of hard work and many years of experience. I began thinking about what differentiates an average, or competent, DBA from a truly exceptional DBA, and the resources that were available to help DBAs progress from the second to the third group.

There was quite a bit of technical information out there – I had contributed a fair bit of it myself – but I couldn't think of a single resource that offered DBAs advice on how to guide and progress through their DBA career. After a lot of thinking, I honed in on the concept of an "Exceptional DBA". What did it mean to be an Exceptional DBA? How did you go about becoming one? What technical skills were required? What other skills were important? I had learnt most of this the hard way, and I decided that I wanted to share what I now knew.

This book is my attempt at doing just that. Its purpose is to provide a "career guide" that will help those individuals who want to become DBAs, or who are now DBAs and want to excel in their job, to become Exceptional DBAs. In the past, if you wanted to become a DBA, you had to jump in and figure it out for yourself, just like I did. There was no guide to help you get started. I hope that this book will become such a guide, helping many people to embark on a successful career as a DBA without wasting a lot of their time figuring out the basics on their own.

Ask yourself the question: why be an average DBA when you can be an exceptional DBA? If you can't think of a good reason why not, and you are

Introduction

willing to put what you learn into action, then this book can help you become an exceptional DBA, and help you excel in your career.

What this Book Covers

This book is not about the technical aspects of being an Exceptional DBA. There are already many good resources available on this topic. This book is a career guide that will show you, step-by-step, specifically what you can do to differentiate yourself from the crowd, so that you can be an Exceptional DBA. While I focus on how to become an Exceptional SQL Server DBA, the advice in this book applies to any DBA, no matter what database software they use.

Specifically, these are the topics I cover:

- Why I Should Become an Exceptional DBA
- Characteristics of the Exceptional DBA
- Specialize: You Can't Do It All
- Hone Your Skill Set
- Is Professional Certification Really Necessary
- Participate in the SQL Server Community
- Manage Your Career, Don't Let it Manage You
- Manage Your Brand Within Your Organization
- Manage Your Online Brand
- Get an Exceptional DBA Job
- Code of Conduct for Exceptional DBAs
- Take Action Now

If you are considering becoming a DBA, or are a DBA and want to be more than an average DBA, this is the book to get you started.

Your Feedback

This book attempts to distil my views on the sorts of skills, attitudes and abilities that mark out an Exceptional DBA, based on my thirteen years in the industry, as a "self-taught" DBA. Along the way, I've learned from many

Introduction

hard-working DBAs, and I describe in this book many of the traits that they displayed.

As such, I hope that it will provide an excellent starting point on your quest to become an Exceptional DBA. However, I also realize that it is just a start. What will make this book an even better guide is your feedback.

Based on your feedback I have updated much of the original material, for this second edition, and added two entirely new chapters; one on how to get an Exceptional DBA job, and one on a Code of Conduct for Exceptional DBAs. However, I'm sure there are still countless ideas, strategies and traits that I've missed out, and I'd like to hear about them. Please send any suggestions, ideas and criticisms that you have to exceptionaldba@red-gate.com. I promise that we will consider and respond to all feedback. If your idea gets incorporated in the next version of this book, we will send you a complimentary copy on publication!

Thanks, and enjoy,

Brad M McGehee

Chapter 1: Why Should I Become an Exceptional DBA?

Before I can tell you why you should become an Exceptional DBA, you must first understand what it means to be an Exceptional DBA. It can involve a lot of hard work, though the rewards can also be commensurately high.

What is an Exceptional DBA?

While I could start out with a dictionary definition, I feel that, ultimately, an Exceptional DBA is defined by his or her actions. So, instead, place yourself in the shoes of a company's DBA, in each of the following scenarios, and consider how you would react:

- You're just about to go home for the day, when the SAN supporting a mission-critical SQL Server cluster fails, bringing the company's systems to a grinding halt.

- It's the weekend and you hear on the radio that a Force 3 hurricane is about to hit your area.

- You've just started your new DBA job, and you find out that the databases don't have any security configured, and backups haven't been made in weeks.

- You notice that a higher than normal number of queries have been hitting the payroll database lately. You find that a sales manager with the company has been running the queries. He has the security rights to perform the queries as a member of the Executive Committee group.

- Word has just come down from the top that an often-delayed database project has to be ready in eight weeks, no excuses. An inexperienced Project Manager is the cause of the delay.

Chapter 1: Why Should I Become an Exceptional DBA?

- The company CFO has been pitched a slick sales presentation on a new BI application that will "save" the company millions of dollars. After some investigation, you're concerned that it will actually end up costing the company tens of thousands of dollars in wasted resources to implement, and that it won't do what it is advertised to do.

There is no single correct response to any of these dilemmas, but in my opinion (and experience), an Exceptional DBA might respond something like as follows:

- **Critical SAN gone down.** You immediately set about contacting all relevant parties and implementing the organization's disaster recovery plan. You don't get any sleep for over 36 hours until the system is back up and running as normal.

- **Hurricane on its way.** You head into work immediately, double-check that all the database backups have been successful and that the company is prepared to move to a backup site should the data center be damaged by the hurricane.

- **No security? No backups.** You immediately go to the IT manager, knock on the door, and explain what the problems are and how you intend to fix them.

- **Suspicious activity on the payroll database.** Despite the security rights he has, you know that the sales manager has no business looking at payroll data, especially for employees that he is not responsible for. You turn over the trace results to your boss.

- **Inexperienced PM and an "impossible" deadline.** You immediately call a meeting of all those involved in the project, and you outline exactly how you will lead the team to a successful completion of the project. You don't care whose "fault" it was, you just want to get the job done on time and done well. The PM might be a little miffed at you, but your manager will recognize and appreciate your leadership.

- **CFO wants to implement a potentially disastrous new BI system.** After a quiet and thorough investigation on the product, you write up a paper discussing the problems with the application and why it won't fit

Chapter 1: Why Should I Become an Exceptional DBA?

well within the organization. You then ask your boss to pass it to the CFO, without asking for any credit for writing the paper. You realize that if the advice comes from your boss, then it will carry more weight with the misinformed CFO.

Did you notice a trend above? While you may not agree with all the examples given above, I think you will notice that Exceptional DBAs are not your typical 40 hour-a-week employees.

An Exceptional DBA is in the Top 10% of Their Profession

There are many different possible ways to define an Exceptional DBA. In this book, an Exceptional DBA is defined as a DBA who is the top ten percent of their profession. These are DBAs who:

- Have outstanding knowledge and experience working with SQL Server.
- Are completely dependable and reliable.
- Willing to work alone or as part as a team.
- Have a "get it done" attitude and don't blame others for problems.
- Fully understand their responsibility to protect the organization's data.
- Have the ability to communicate effectively in writing and verbally.
- Shares his or her knowledge with the co-workers and the SQL Server community.

This is not a description of a fantasy DBA Super Hero, but a description of the many hard-working DBAs I have met over the course of my career. Exceptional DBAs can be found almost everywhere, and you can become one too.

Why Bother?

Becoming an Exceptional DBA takes hard work, so the question you may be asking yourself now is: "Is it worth all the time and effort it takes to become an Exceptional DBA?" To be honest, this is a decision you have to make; I

Chapter 1: Why Should I Become an Exceptional DBA?

can't make it for you. You must weigh the pros and cons of becoming an Exceptional DBA and decide for yourself if the benefits outweigh their costs. As you may have already guessed, the 90% of DBAs who aren't Exceptional DBAs don't believe the benefits outweigh the costs; otherwise they wouldn't be in the bottom 90%. However, I beg to disagree with them, and I think you should too. For example, consider the following benefits of becoming an Exceptional DBA.

Direct Personal Benefits

DBAs are among the highest paid IT professionals. According to Salary.Com, as of April 2009, the top 10% of all DBAs earn at least USD $106,142 a year, plus benefits. This is a national average of U.S.-based jobs, and the actual amount will vary depending on many factors, including number of years of experience, the size of the company, the location of the company, DBA specialty area, and more. I know many DBAs who make over $100,000 a year, and this goal is not as unattainable as you might assume.

> **NOTE:**
> For comparison purposes, according to Salary.Com, mid-range DBAs make between $62,944 to $106,142 per year, mid-range Software Developers make between $58,156 and $84,975 per year, and mid-range Network Administrators make between $46,894 and $77,249 per year. Which of these pay ranges would you prefer to be in?

Although being fairly paid for a challenging job is important, I don't know of any Exceptional DBAs who are just doing it for the money. Most do it for the satisfaction of working in a technically challenging and ever-changing environment. Being an Exceptional DBA affords you the opportunity to keep on the cutting edge of technology. Many new software development innovations are the result of figuring out how to make applications work well with databases – and I don't think we will see any slowing of technology any time soon.

If that's not enough, consider these additional benefits:
- According to the United States Bureau of Labor Statistics, DBA jobs will "grow much faster than average" compared to other types of jobs,

Chapter 1: Why Should I Become an Exceptional DBA?

- through 2016. See http://www.bls.gov/oco/ocos042.htm for more information.
- DBAs are needed almost everywhere, small towns and large cities alike, affording you the opportunity to live almost anywhere you what to live.
- Often, being a DBA affords you the opportunity to travel, assuming you want to. This is especially true if you work as a consultant and travel to client sites. I know many DBAs who travel internationally on a regular basis.
- Most Exceptional DBAs have excellent self-confidence and self-esteem. Most people don't start a particular career for this specific purpose, but self-confidence and self-esteem are benefits that any exceptional person accrues when they perform a job well.

Benefits on the Job

As an Exceptional DBA, you generally receive more peer respect, more credibility, and more influence in your organization. Being respected by your peers is a great feeling, especially if you are part of a larger team that works well together. Because of the importance of DBAs to organizations, not only is their job held in higher regard than many other IT positions, they are often the last to be laid off, should layoffs occur.

In times of economic downturn it is natural for all IT professionals to be concerned about their job security. Although DBAs tend to remain in relatively high demand during such periods, compared to other IT positions, nobody is immune from layoffs. There is just too much uncertainty to be able to predict how any one business will perform, or even survive, during such troublesome times.

Rather than sit around worrying about the state of the economy, or losing your job, my advice is to redouble your efforts to learn new skills, and work your way towards becoming an Exceptional DBA. If you do so, you can make yourself so valuable at your current job that they can't afford to be without you. Even if the worst happens and you get laid off anyway, the time you invested in improving your skills will make finding a new position much easier. In short, my advice is to invest in yourself and your career, especially in times of recession. It won't cost you anything but time, and it will pay huge dividends your entire career.

Chapter 1: Why Should I Become an Exceptional DBA?

DBAs often have good opportunities for job growth and advancement, whether they are looking to stay with the same company, change companies, or start their own company. Becoming an Exceptional DBA, along with honing your management skills, can be a stepping-stone for becoming a CIO.

Benefits to your Organization

Most employees don't think in terms of how valuable they can be to their own organization. This is a shame, because in the real world, more often than not, when you help your organization become more successful, you also become more successful. Many people are sour on how their organization treats them, which affects their ability to perform well. You need to learn how to ignore this negative feeling and, instead, focus on what you can do to help the organization. The rewards can be plentiful. If your organization doesn't work this way, then you need to find one that does.

At some point in your career, you may become the leader of your own organization. Don't you want to create a great environment for your employees, one that reaches out to meet their needs, instead of just focusing on what you want? The more you help others, the more they help you. This is one of the fundamental principles of all business and personal success.

Summary: The Road to Becoming an Exceptional DBA

Now that you have seen what an Exceptional DBA is, and some of the many benefits that accrue from being an Exceptional DBA, are you ready to find out how to accomplish this goal? Great, because the rest of this book will show you exactly what you need to do to become an Exceptional DBA.

Chapter 2: Characteristics of the Exceptional DBA

Chapter 1 touched upon some of the common characteristics that define an Exceptional DBA, and why you might want to make the extra effort to become one. In this chapter, I'd like to expand on this discussion and explore in more detail the characteristics that define an Exceptional DBA. Few DBAs will have all these characteristics, but the best DBAs will have most of them.

As you follow the discussion in this chapter, you'll probably find yourself mentally assessing the degree to which you possess a given characteristic. A mental comparison like this is good. It helps you to determine what your strengths are and where your weaknesses lie.

If you find that you don't possess very many of these characteristics right now, don't panic. Keep in mind that most Exceptional DBAs take many years to develop these characteristics and that nobody exhibits all these characteristics all the time. After all, none of us is perfect. Simply regard the characteristics that you don't currently possess as goals that you can work towards over time. Each of these characteristics can be learned when you set your mind to it, just as you have the ability to learn a new SQL Server skill.

Enjoys Technology

If you are reading this book, then I think I can reasonably assume that you already enjoy technology, a key trait of all Exceptional DBAs and IT professionals. The only reason I mention this obvious point is that I occasionally run into DBAs who actually don't appear to enjoy working with technology. For example, at conferences I often sit at breakfast or lunch tables with attendees who I don't know. I ask them about their job and why they are attending the conference. It is always a shock to hear somebody tell me that the only reason they are at the conference is because their boss made them attend. The only advice I can really offer these people is this: find yourself a new career.

Chapter 2: Characteristics of the Exceptional DBA

Enjoys Challenge

A challenge is an ambiguous concept. That which presents a challenge to one person may be a slam-dunk to another. For example, writing a Transact-SQL script might be a daunting task to some DBAs, but for others, it is something they can do almost in their sleep.

Every DBA faces a different set of challenges in their daily work, and it is not necessarily the ability to respond immediately to a given technical challenge (for example, by dashing off a SQL script) that sets apart the exceptional DBA. It is more their attitude toward challenges that makes the distinction.

Here are some examples that might explain what I mean:

- You have just found out that management wants to upgrade all 350 SQL Servers instances from SQL Server 2005 to SQL Server 2008, by the end of the quarter. Rather than immediately raise objections, the Exceptional DBA will scope out the project, create a plan, and put it into effect as soon as possible. If the DBA determines, after scoping, that it is impossible to complete the job in time given current resources, then he will determine what additional resources are needed and present his findings to his manager.
- A SQL Server instance that has been running smoothly for months suddenly starts running slowly. You are getting lots of phone calls from unhappy users. The Exceptional DBA would immediately gather and analyze the relevant information, make an educated guess as to the cause of the problem, identify a potential solution, then test it to see if it works. If the first try does not succeed, the Exceptional DBA continues to carry out research, seeks more information, and tests potential solutions until the problem is resolved.
- A new project manager for the company seems to think that you work for him, when that is not the case. He has assigned you a number of new projects without even consulting you; projects that you don't have time to do. Once the Exceptional DBA discovers this "people problem", he goes to his manager to seek an explanation and works out the matter in a mutually agreeable way, with this manager and the project manager.

Chapter 2: Characteristics of the Exceptional DBA

Notice that in none of these scenarios did the Exceptional DBA complain about the challenges posed, but instead jumped immediately into resolving the challenge, not putting it off or hoping it would go away on its own.

Exceptional DBAs regard challenges as opportunities to learn something new; to do something different. They aren't afraid of challenges, they look forward to them. In many ways, challenges are just a part of the normal routine of being a DBA.

Enjoys Problem Solving

Every day, DBAs solve problems. They may be as simple as determining why a backup failed, or as complex as creating a disaster recovery plan for a large on-line merchant. The Exceptional DBA regards problems as a new challenge (see previous trait); a puzzle to solve. This is why they come to work, because each day is different and challenging. If they don't have new problems to solve, they get bored. In other words, the Exceptional DBA enjoys the process of problem solving. For example:

- 8:01 AM: An end-user calls, reporting a deadlock in her application.
- 8:08 AM: An end-user calls complaining about a slow-running report.
- 8:14 AM: You check the backup records for last night and discover that one server ran out of disk space, causing the backup to fail.
- 8:20 AM: You get an e-mail from your manager for a meeting that is to start at 9:00 AM.
- 8:21 AM: A network staffer shows up at your desk, asking why network utilization spiked at 3:30 AM on one of the SQL Servers.
- 8:33 AM: The end-user calls you again, asking if you have fixed the slow running report yet.
- 8:40 AM: You free up space and initiate a backup on the server that had a backup failure last night.
- 8:51 AM: You solve the slow-running report problem.
- 9:00 AM: You attend the meeting your boss just called.

The above example of an hour in the life of an Exceptional DBA is not unusual. Often, new problems arise so fast that you can't keep up with them. While this may wear out many people, the Exceptional DBA thrives on this kind of activity. Sure, there are times when it is nice to have some peace and

Chapter 2: Characteristics of the Exceptional DBA

quiet to catch up, but most Exceptional DBAs prefer to be busy most of the time.

While Exceptional DBAs enjoy problem solving, they also realize the following important points:

1. Not every problem can be solved.
2. Some problems can be solved after time spent troubleshooting, and can wait.
3. Some problems can be solved after time spent troubleshooting, but need to be fixed now.

When cases of type 3 arise, the Exceptional DBA has no issue with asking for help. The Exceptional DBA is comfortable with the idea that they don't know all the answers and that, if time is a problem, calling in help sooner rather than later is the best approach to take. This could mean posting a question on a forum or on Twitter, calling Microsoft SQL Server Product Support, or whichever other route is open to them in order to find the answer they need, quickly.

Good with Details

For a DBA, the job is all about details. First, and foremost, the Exceptional DBA must have the detailed, in-depth technical skills they need to perform their daily work. There is no such thing as an "almost perfect" backup or a "fairly good" transaction. In most cases, something either works or it doesn't, and the Exceptional DBA must be intimately familiar with the many and detailed steps required to perform their work.

Second, Exceptional DBAs must be very thorough and meticulous as they perform their work. For example, if a DBA wants to set up security on his or her servers, to prevent any possibility of unauthorized access, they must carefully sort through the many possible ways security could be breached, and protect against each one.

Third, Exceptional DBAs need to be exhaustive and comprehensive when performing their work. For example, when creating a disaster recovery plan for an organization, the DBA must consider every possible disaster, determine how it might affect his or her servers, and develop a plan to minimize the consequences if the disaster occurs.

Chapter 2: Characteristics of the Exceptional DBA

I am not sure that I would list "enjoying details" as a required characteristic of being an exceptional DBA, but dealing effectively with details is critical.

Embraces Change

As ironic as it sounds, one of the only constants in the career of the Exceptional DBA, is change. While DBAs many not see change every day, changes big and small occur frequently, often with little or no warning. For example:

- A new SQL Server instance needs to be installed and configured.
- Another SQL Server needs its hardware upgraded.
- You have been told that all existing SQL Server user access has to be audited starting the first of the year.
- Patches have to be added to all SQL Server instances on a monthly basis.
- Your current manager quits and you have to "break in" a new one.
- A new ERP system is to be implemented in the company by the end of the year.
- Your company buys another company, and you must integrate the data within the next 90 days.
- Your company goes out of business and you lose your job.

Sometimes it can be fun, and other times disheartening, but the Exceptional DBA regards change as inevitable. Instead of fighting it, they embrace it, and do the best they can with what is given to them.

Enjoys Learning

If you don't love to learn, there is no way you can keep up with the constant changes in database and related technology. Some general skills, such as problem solving, only have to be learned once. Other skills, such as technology-specific skills, have to be continuously relearned as that technology changes and evolves. The only way to keep up is to become a lifelong learner. You need to take as much time as you can find not only to keep your current skills up to date, but also to add skills to your repertoire.

Chapter 2: Characteristics of the Exceptional DBA

The Exceptional DBA realizes the need for constant learning and includes it as part of his or her schedule. For example, scheduling in time for learning a new SQL Server skill, reading a professional publication, checking out the latest SQL Server blogs, attending classes or user group meetings, or even attending national conferences, are all ways the Exceptional DBA can keep up.

For the Exceptional DBA, learning is a part of his or her lifestyle and job, not just something that has to be "squeezed in" only when necessary.

Accepts Responsibility

Exceptional DBAs not only accept responsibility for their assigned tasks, but also for their actions. For example, if the DBA is responsible for safeguarding the data integrity of an organization, then the DBA will take all prudent steps required to see that the data is protected.

If that same DBA makes a mistake that causes some data corruption, then he should immediately stand up and admit to the mistake, and not try to minimize his involvement. Besides taking responsibility for their actions, Exceptional DBAs will also offer solutions to prevent the same problem from recurring.

Maintains Professionalism

Professionalism on the job covers many different areas, but it really comes done to a single idea: respect for others and the organization you work for. Another way to look at professionalism is via the old adage: treat others as you would like them to treat you.

Here are some examples.

- In a meeting, you listen to other's ideas and consider them, even if you don't agree with them. You don't ignore the ideas or, even worse, tell everyone how bad their ideas are.
- If you have been asked to participate in a project, and you just don't have the time to participate, don't say yes and then not participate. Be

- upfront and honest, telling the person you just don't have the time right now.
- You see a co-worker having a problem that you know how to solve. You volunteer to help out, sharing your knowledge. You don't let the co-worker fail when you could have helped.
- If a particular person in upper manager is an idiot, you don't need to share your feelings with others. Most people have probably figured this out for themselves.
- When your organization is going in a direction you feel is wrong, speak up! Offer well-considered opinions and options. If your opinions are ignored, go along with the new direction or find a new job; don't try to sabotage the project or talk badly about it to others.
- You dislike one of your co-workers, but instead of going after him or her, you try to reconcile your differences. If you can't, you still treat them with respect.

The examples could go on and on, but I think you understand how professionalism works. It's all a matter of respect.

Trustworthy

As a DBA, you are often privy to many company secrets. You have access to data that could potentially harm individuals, or your organization, should it be made public. This knowledge carries with it a heavy responsibility. From the organization's point-of-view, it is your responsibility to protect it, insuring that only those who need access to the data have it. If the data is lawful then this is an easy responsibility to uphold. You just don't share it with any person who is not authorized to know about it.

On the other hand, you are bound by legal responsibilities outside of your organization. Although rare, you may, on occasion, discover data about unlawful activities. This may require you to investigate the best options you have available, such as contacting an attorney, asking advice from a trusted friend, or even quitting your job if aren't comfortable with the situation. You are not required to be a hero in these occasions, but you are expected to meet your legal obligations as a citizen.

Chapter 2: Characteristics of the Exceptional DBA

Another aspect of being trustworthy is being honest. Just as you should be honest in your personal life, you also need to be honest in your work life. Yes, there can be justification for the occasional white lie (you tell your boss that his new tie really looks nice, even though it doesn't), but when it comes to substantial issues, honestly is the only option. If you are asked how long it will take for a particular project to be completed, offer your honest advice. Don't tell the person what you think he wants to hear. If you are asked to do something you don't want to do, don't say you will, then not do it.

The Exceptional DBA needs to develop a reputation beyond reproach.

Dependable

Being dependable is much like being trustworthy. It is a sign of who you are and how you interact with others. Some examples include:

- **You do what you say you are going to do**. If something out of your control prevents you from doing what you said you would do, then you let the people involved know about it as soon as possible.
- **You do what you are expected to do**. If it is your responsibility, for example, to write a budget every fiscal year, then you perform that task as expected, and turn in the budget on time.
- **You are punctual**. You show up to work on time, and you show up to meetings on time.

Not only do you do the tasks you agreed to do, and are expected of you, but you do them well, and you complete them on time. The Exceptional DBA needs to have at least a "four nines" dependability level, just as you expect your SQL Servers to have "four nines" up time, or more.

Hard-Working

In most cases, Exceptional DBAs work hard, and spend a lot of time at work. They are often expected to get a task done "now," and to work as long as it takes to get it done. They are often also "on call", and will be expected to come to work at any hour of the day if a problem needs to be fixed.

Chapter 2: Characteristics of the Exceptional DBA

I have often worked long days (36 hours in one stretch was my record), come into the office at weekends, and taken phone calls in the middle of the night. Of course, I always try to be a proactive DBA in order to minimize as many problems as possible, but there is just no way to envision and avoid every potential problem.

If you prefer an 8:00 AM to 5:00 PM job, then being a production DBA is probably not your calling. On the other hand, there are some DBA specialties that require little or no on-call duty, such as Database Designer, Developer, Report Writer, or trainer.

Can Work Well Independently or in a Team

As a DBA, you will sometimes work by yourself, and other times as part of a larger team. You need to be able to do both well, if you want to be an Exceptional DBA.

The Exceptional DBA will encounter many times when he or she works alone. This could include creating scripts, monitoring server performance, troubleshooting problems, or writing documentation. The Exceptional DBA is able to work quietly, alone, without the need to constantly interact with others.

Conversely, the Exceptional DBA will often work as part of a team. This might be a team of production DBAs who oversee a large SQL Server farm, or maybe the production DBA is part of a development team, creating an in-house application. In these cases, there will need to be a lot of communication by everyone on the team, in order for everything to run smoothly.

I would like to make a personal observation here. Many DBAs I know are…how can I say this politely…"independent" types. By being independent, I mean that they think they are smarter than most everyone else at their organization, and that only they know the best way to manage SQL Server, or to write SQL Server-based applications. While it is great to be a smart DBA, being a smart DBA does not make you an Exceptional DBA. By being independent, many DBAs sabotage their careers because they are not good team players.

Chapter 2: Characteristics of the Exceptional DBA

Manages Time Well

The study of economics is all about learning how to find a balance between people who have unlimited needs and wants, and a physical world with only limited resources. The same can be said about the work of the DBA. Most organizations have a seemingly insatiable desire to assign DBAs (and all IT staff, for that matter) a huge amount of work. On the other hand, the DBA only has a limited amount of time, and physical resources, in which to produce the work. The result can be a state of constant conflict between the DBA and the rest of the organization.

This situation is further complicated by the many warring factions within an organization, each one feeling that their needs are more important than the needs of other factions. For example, one project may need the use of two DBAs for six months, and another project may need a DBA for three months. If the organization only has two full time DBAs for all production and development work, and these projects overlap, this presents a problem. Technically speaking, it is up to the DBA's manager to find the right balance. However, in the real world, this often is not the case, and DBAs often ends up with more work that they can realistically accomplish.

There is no easy way to resolve this problem. Having a very understanding manager will help a lot, but the only real choice for the DBA is to be as efficient as he or she can be, making the most of the available time and resources. For example:

- By proactively following **SQL Server best practices,** the DBA should be able to minimize the occurrence of performance issues and many other SQL Server-related problems, and at the same time help to boost availability.
- By taking advantage of **third-party tools,** the DBA should be able to perform many routine tasks much faster than they could if performing them manually. If third-party tools are not available, then the DBA should have a complete grasp of all the tools that are included with SQL Server.
- By minimizing participation in unnecessary meetings or social networking, the DBA will have more time to do actual work.

Chapter 2: Characteristics of the Exceptional DBA

- By becoming **more knowledgeable about SQL Server,** less time should be necessary to perform many tasks, or to troubleshoot problems when they do occur.
- By **scheduling tasks and projects,** the DBA knows what has to be done, and can better juggle tasks when necessary.

The Exceptional DBA realizes that he or she can only offer a finite amount of work in a given amount of time. To maximize the work-to-time ratio, the Exceptional DBA carefully manages time, focusing on what is important and ignoring what is unimportant. He or she also looks for every possible way to extend their capacity to work, by making full use of productivity tools.

Can Communicate Effectively, Both Orally and Verbally

Whether you like it or not, DBAs must be effective communicators. Unfortunately, the art of good communication is not taught in most schools, and many DBAs find themselves in uncomfortable positions because of their lack of communication skills. Here are some examples of where good communications skills are needed by the DBA:

- Making a PowerPoint presentation at a company meeting.
- Convincing your manager that a SQL Server needs more RAM.
- Writing hardware specifications for a new SQL Server.
- As a DBA consultant, making a sales presentation to a potential client.
- Writing a proposal to purchase a third-party tool to administer your SQL Servers.
- Documenting SQL Server development best practices for use by developers.
- Writing a disaster recovery document.
- Creating and writing a budget proposal.
- Teaching an in-house class to other DBAs or developers.
- Speaking at a conference or user's group meeting.
- Sharing information in a public forum.
- Writing a SQL Server or personal blog.

Chapter 2: Characteristics of the Exceptional DBA

- Writing articles for SQL Server community website and publications.
- Writing a resume.

While a typical DBA may not participate in all of the above activities, the Exceptional DBA often participates in most of them. Becoming an effective communicator is one of the secrets of becoming an Exceptional DBA. After all, if you can't communicate how good you are to others, how can you ever be recognized as an Exceptional DBA?

Listens Well

An important part of becoming a good communicator is being a good listener. Many people confuse "hearing" with "listening." To listen well means not only to hear what another person is saying, but also to understand what the person is saying, and why they are saying it. Consider the following four examples.

Example 1: A user calls up and tells you that SQL Server is down. If that is all you heard, and you don't ask any questions, you would hang up and then go check out the server to see why it is down. When I hear such a comment, I automatically assume that the user is not telling me everything (generally not on purpose, but usually because of a lack of knowledge), so I ask follow-up questions. For example, I might ask: Can you tell me what is not working? What application are you using? When did the problem first occur? Instead of just acting blindly on the information you hear, ask questions, dig deeper and make sure you really understand what the other person is trying to say.

Example 2: For the third time in a week, a new employee calls you up, asking when his SQL Server user ID and password will be effective. And for the third time you tell him that he is set up and can log in anytime he wants. Again, he says that he can't log in. If all you do is repeat yourself each time the user asks the same question, the odds are that you won't solve the problem. Again, you must ask very specific questions so that you fully understand the user's situation. For example, ask the user exactly what screen he is at. Ask what is on the screen. Ask him what he is typing in, and in what parts of the screen. Or if you have to, visit the user and watch him try to log in. The problem could be that he is at the wrong screen, or he is using all

Chapter 2: Characteristics of the Exceptional DBA

uppercase letters, or perhaps he was given an incorrect password. Who knows, unless you take the effort to get to the real cause of the problem?

Example 3: Your manager tells you that you will be reassigned to the development department for a new project, and to show up next week to see the new project manager. If that is all you hear, and know, this can create a lot of anxiety for you, as you don't know what is really going on. To find out, ask questions, find out why you are being reassigned, for how long, and when you will be going back to your regular duties. If you are still worried about this move once you've find out the details, then let your manager know that you are apprehensive and ask even more questions in order to resolve the issue.

Example 4: You are a consultant and are talking with client's end users, finding out what their needs are. If all you hear is that they need some sales reports, this is not very useful. You need to know exactly what data they need, where the data is at, how often they need the data, how the data will be used, and on and on. The more specific the questions, the better the answers will be. I am sure you know of many cases where the needs of users have not been met by developers because the developers never really listened to what the users wanted in the first place.

Exceptional DBAs know that what people say is not always what they really mean. They make an extra effort to make sure they really understand what the person needs, and then take the appropriate action. Keep in mind that not everyone is a good communicator, and that you may have to help others communicate with you.

Realistic

I have seen this over and over again in my career. A new DBA starts with a company, all gung-ho about making his or her mark. He offers lots of ideas and advice, but nobody really listens, and he eventually becomes discouraged. Eventually, he either ends up quitting and finding different work, or staying and ending up like Wally, the cynical engineer in the Dilbert comic strip.

In another case, I know of a DBA who expected everybody to do things his way. When this did not work out for him, he blamed the organization and his co-workers. As far as he was concerned, everyone else was the root cause of his problems. He became a complainer and whiner, and nobody wanted to work with him.

Chapter 2: Characteristics of the Exceptional DBA

DBAs must have realistic expectations about their job, and they must come to grips with the reality that no job will meet all of their expectations. Not even self-employment will necessarily meet 100% of one's expectations. Every job has its good and bad points. The Exceptional DBA understands this and accepts it. When things don't work out as planned, the Exceptional DBA learns from the situation and moves on. I don't necessarily mean moving to another job, just moving on with their job and life in general, and not letting small problems become big problems.

Of course, there will be cases when a job is so bad that you have no choice but to leave, but this is rare, assuming you had realistic expectations in the first place. If you find that you are bouncing from one job to another, you may want to reevaluate your job expectations, and try to make them a little more realistic.

Flexible

Being flexible in your approach to your job is really just an extension of being realistic about your job. In other words, the job of the DBA changes over time, and you have to be flexible and be willing to change as the job changes.

The following are fairly typical examples of where some flexibility is required on the behalf of the DBA:

- You have been hired to work on DBA development projects, but the needs of the organization have changed and now you are needed to do production DBA work instead.
- You are used to managing 50 SQL Servers, but then another DBA quits and the company needs to cut back on operating expenses, so they do not refill the position. You end up managing 100 SQL Servers.
- Your manager asks you to create a BI application. This is something that you have never done before, but the company can't justify the cost of hiring a consultant, so you have been elected to complete the project.

Flexibility is important on a day-to-day basis, as well as when dealing with the "bigger" challenges. For example, when you came to work today, you might have planned on writing some needed documentation, but instead you find out that you needed to help a developer tune a poorly-performing query.

Chapter 2: Characteristics of the Exceptional DBA

Or maybe you had planned on installing a new SQL Server instance, but a blocking problem arises that you need to investigate right away, because users are complaining about not getting their work done.

In short, the Exceptional DBA realizes that things change, and that he or she has to adapt to the situation at hand.

Patient

It takes a half hour for the new service pack to install. It takes six minutes to reboot the server. The query takes 16 minutes to run before it finishes. It takes an hour to explain to a new developer the organization's best practices for writing stored procedures. The backup takes four hours to complete.

The DBA is often faced with one request after another, often in a rapid-fire sort of way. On the other hand, many DBA tasks take time, lots of time, wasted time. Sometimes the waiting can be used to perform other tasks, and other times it can't. However you look at it, DBAs end up spending a lot of time waiting for something to happen before they can proceed with their next task.

The Exceptional DBA learns to be a patient person, to expect that tasks will take longer than they had hoped. Moreover, they build this into their schedules, as they are realistic and know that waiting is just a part of the job of the DBA. Exceptional DBAs also take this time to relax, to find a little quiet time out of an often-turbulent day.

Persistent

"If at first you don't succeed, try, try again." This old adage is well suited to the DBA profession, where patience and persistence is most definitely required. I can't count the number of times I have worked to resolve a problem, hour after hour, sometimes day after day, until it is resolved. The problem might be technical, such as speeding up a slow query; or it might be a resource problem, such as getting management to buy you faster servers. In any case, Exceptional DBAs are almost always persistent DBAs. They don't give up when faced with challenges; they tackle them head on until they have succeeded.

Chapter 2: Characteristics of the Exceptional DBA

Enthusiastic

All of the Exceptional DBAs I know have a passion for their jobs. The really enjoy their work, and it is a big part of their lives. The reasons they are passionate vary widely. It may be because they enjoy technology, and solving problems, or because they feel they are providing a worthwhile service in the marketplace. It may be that they like to share their knowledge with others, or like to be creative in their work. It may be because they work for a great organization or have great co-workers. Each Exceptional DBA has their own reasons why they enjoy their work, making it hard to describe all of them here.

Not only does enthusiasm help a DBA become an Exceptional DBA, being an Exceptional DBA helps fuel even more enthusiasm. This is a positive feedback loop than can contribute to a very rewarding, lifelong career.

Self-Confident

Self-confidence helps the Exceptional DBA reach his or her goals, and is also the reward that the Exceptional DBA receives for a job well done. If you are seeking to become an Exceptional DBA, you need to start out with clear, simple goals. Once you have attained these, you can set yourself additional, more difficult goals. If you proceed slowly like this, you will begin to develop more confidence in your abilities. Moreover, the more self-confidence you gain, the easier it will be for you to continue on your path to becoming an Exceptional DBA.

Thinks Before Acting

How many times have you seen a novice DBA read about some new tip or technique, and then immediately try it out on a production server? Ouch! This happens much more often than you may think, and can contribute to a multitude of problems, ranging from slower performance to bringing a server down. Exceptional DBAs, on the other hand, always think before they act. For example, if a DBA is troubleshooting a slowly performing query and decides to create a new index to boost its performance, he will it try out first

Chapter 2: Characteristics of the Exceptional DBA

on a test box. If performance increases as he predicted, and there are no negative consequences, only then will he roll out the index to production. Before making even the smallest of changes, the Exceptional DBA must always think carefully through the potential consequences of his actions.

Mature

Over the years I have met many Exceptional DBAs, and perhaps their most common shared characteristic is that they tend to be mature, responsible adults. They tend to have strong family values, many of them are religious, and many are community volunteers. In other words, they are the kind of people that other people admire and trust. They are the pillars of the community. The more you think about it, the more this makes sense. Being a DBA is all about being dependable and trustworthy. I don't know if mature people tend to seek out DBA jobs, or if organizations prefer to hire mature people in DBA roles. In any event, there is a definite correlation.

Chapter 2: Characteristics of the Exceptional DBA

Summary: Assess your Strengths and Weaknesses

Now that you seen the characteristics that define most Exceptional DBAs, how well do you measure up? Do you know what your strengths and weakness are? While some people will be able to make a mental tally of where they stand, others may prefer to write them down on paper. For example, take a piece of paper and draw a line down the center of it. On the left hand side write your strengths, and on the right hand side write down your weaknesses.

Once you are done with your assessment, consider which characteristics are your strengths, which ones need work, and which ones you might consider skipping. Remember, most Exceptional DBAs have taken many years to develop these characteristics, and that not all Exceptional DBAs have all these strengths.

In later chapters, we will talk more about how you can develop these strengths, including what actions you can take to attain specific goals.

Chapter 3: Specialize (You can't do it all)

In this chapter, we are going to look at the many different types of job functions that a DBA might be asked to perform. The list is a long one, and if you're an experienced DBA you'll probably be familiar with most, if not all of them.

If you look around DBA job postings you'll notice that there are almost as many different specifications for a DBA's job as there are DBAs. Very few DBAs can master every potential facet of SQL Server, so the Exceptional DBA will generally choose to specialize in certain areas. Later in this chapter, we'll take a look at the different areas in which a DBA might decide to focus.

What exactly is a DBA?

A DBA (Database Administrator) is an IT Professional who is responsible for the ongoing operations of an organization's databases and the applications that access the databases. The position encompasses many different job functions and job titles, and these vary widely from one organization to the next. In short, there is no "standard job description" to which a DBA can refer. This is partly because the job title of DBA doesn't have a long history, and partly because the functions of the DBA are quickly evolving.

If you were to ask ten different DBAs what their duties were, you would get ten different answers. In one job, the organization may need a DBA to manage existing SQL Server instances, while another organization may want a Transact-SQL and C# developer, another might want an SSIS expert, while another may be want a DBA who knows how to design databases.

Unfortunately, many advertised DBA positions don't list the required skills, making it hard for you to decide if a particular DBA-type job opening will meet your interests and skill set. This happens in large part because there is poor communication between the person doing the hiring and the person writing the job ad. If you are not sure what skills an organization is looking for, you may want to call or e-mail the organization for more information.

Chapter 3: Specialize (You can't do it all)

There is no point in applying for a job that doesn't meet your job skills or interests.

This happened to me once. I applied for a job for what appeared to be a production DBA, doing exactly the kind of work I had been doing. After applying and then going in for an interview, I was asked about all kinds of aspects of DBA work that I was not particularly familiar with. After about thirty minutes of being interviewed, I told the interviewer that the job, as described in the interview, did not meet my job skills or interests. If I had only spent a little more time asking questions upfront, I would have saved myself a lot of wasted time.

An A-to-Z List of Typical DBA Tasks

DBAs perform many different tasks. So many, in fact, that it is hard to categorize them all. Below, I have compiled a list, in alphabetical order, of some of the more common tasks you find DBAs performing. This list is by no means comprehensive. My goal is to cover the most common tasks so that you are familiar with them, and can better understand what DBAs do. Also, keep in mind that many of these job functions overlap.

Archiving Data

Data grows over time and can become costly to store and difficult to manage. In addition, having more data tends to exasperate performance problems. As a DBA, you must monitor data size and growth, and determine the best way to store it. In some cases, this may include archiving seldom-used data in another database or server, or it might even mean purging data that is no longer needed.

Often you will find that your choices are limited, as company policy and government regulations can restrict how and where you store data.

Chapter 3: Specialize (You can't do it all)

Attending Meetings

Most DBAs I know hate attending meetings because they can't use that time to do the work they really like, or need, to do. However, meetings are a fact of working life and, if used wisely, aren't necessarily a waste of time. With correct planning and preparation, meetings are great opportunities for improving communications.

Auditing

An emerging task of the DBA is to identify which users are accessing, inserting, updating, or deleting data, and when. Auditing might only be necessary for limited time periods, for specific users, for very specific data, or it might be required 24/7 for all data. While performing this task, DBAs often have to work with both internal and external auditors. In one case, the organization I worked for sent in a team of external auditors to audit our IT operations. Unfortunately, the outside auditors were fresh out of college and had no IT experience whatsoever. I ended up having to teach them what SQL Server was used for and how it worked.

Application Integration

While most organizations use third-party applications, very few of these applications work in isolation. In other words, disparate applications have to be made to talk to one another, often using the database as the means to share data. DBAs often get involved in figuring out the best way to integrate applications. This may include creating custom applications, Transact-SQL scripts, or SSIS packages.

Backup and Recovery

One of the most fundamental aspects of the DBA's job is to protect the organization's data. This includes making periodic backups of data and keeping it safe from accidental or intentional destruction. In addition, a well-developed recovery plan needs to be implemented and tested so that when problems do arise, data can be restored quickly. One of the biggest mistakes novice DBAs make is not testing their backups. Just because a database is

Chapter 3: Specialize (You can't do it all)

backed up, it does not guarantee that it can be restored. Exceptional DBAs not only ensure that backups are made, but that they can be restored successfully.

Business Intelligence/Data Warehousing

One of the fastest growing areas for the DBA is Business Intelligence (BI) and data warehousing. This is because more and more organizations are seeking to mine all the information they can, in order to make better business decisions. This area has become so complex that many DBAs specialize in just this one discipline. If you are looking for a fast-growing, high-paying career option, and you like to take on complex tasks, then you might want to give this DBA discipline a close look.

Capacity Planning

In most organizations, the number and size of databases grows rapidly. It is the responsibility of the DBA to watch data growth, and plan how best to deal with it. This may include archiving it, increasing the size of current hardware, or adding new hardware.

Change Management

SQL Server configurations, database schema, Transact-SQL code, and many other facets of the application ecosystem, change over time. It is often the responsibility to the DBA to perform impact analysis before changes are made, implement changes, test changes, and document them.

For example, a common task for DBAs is to move changes made to development servers to test servers for testing and, once testing is done, to move the changes to production. This can become a very complex process because many dependencies are involved and, if a single mistake is made, it can cause productions systems to fail. Fortunately, there are many good third-party tools that can be used to make this job easier and more failsafe.

Database Application Development

Many DBAs are really application developers who specialize in writing code to directly access SQL Server. While this is most commonly done using Transact-SQL and stored procedures, it can involve writing other code that is

Chapter 3: Specialize (You can't do it all)

used to access SQL Server data. Many DBAs decide to make this their area of specialty, because an in-depth knowledge of development is required to be a good database applications developer.

Data Modeling and Database Design

The foundation of all efficient and scalable databases is good database design. DBAs often create database designs by performing needs / requirements analysis, creating a logical model, and then implementing the physical model. In larger organizations, there may be DBAs who specialize in database design.

Developing and Maintaining Best Practices

Exceptional DBAs are proactive in their work, and one of the best ways to be proactive is to develop sound database best practices and to implement them. The better organized and managed the database operations, the more efficient they will be. Ideally, an organization's best practices will be documented for all to read and follow.

High Availability

A DBA needs to ensure that his or her databases are available to users when they need access to data. There are many different ways to help ensure high availability, including use of log shipping, clustering, database mirroring, and other technologies. Because of the very specialized knowledge required for high availability techniques, many DBAs focus in this area.

Installing, Configuring, Patching and Upgrading SQL Server Software

One of the most time-consuming of all database tasks is installing, configuring, patching and upgrading SQL Server instances. While installing and configuring new instances is relatively straight-forward, it can be time-consuming. On the other hand, patching or upgrading is complicated by the fact that it must be done during a planned down time, and there is always the risk that any change made to a SQL Server instance will cause it to malfunction or fail. To prevent this possibility, a lot of testing, and backout

Chapter 3: Specialize (You can't do it all)

planning, has to be done before changes are made to production. Installing and Configuring Hardware

In some organizations, hardware (the server and I/O subsystem) is handled by dedicated hardware technicians. In others, the DBA is responsible for building, installing, and configuring their own hardware. In addition, DBAs may also perform regular hardware troubleshooting and maintenance.

Load Balancing

Over time, the load put on individual databases changes. DBAs are responsible for monitoring workloads and figuring out how to maximize hardware resources to get the best SQL Server performance. This may involve moving a database from a busy server to a less busy server. It can also involve server consolidation or virtualization.

Maintaining Documentation

Writing and maintaining documentation is probably the most boring and loathed task that a DBA will encounter. However boring it is, it is still a critical part of the DBA's job. If you don't document, then there is no easy way to rebuild the current infrastructure should major problems arise. Here's a tip of new DBAs: if you want to make a good impression on your manager, and the other DBAs in your team, volunteer to write the documentation. Not only will you get to learn your organization's systems, you will also demonstrate to everyone that you are a team player who is not afraid of work.

Managing Managers

A manager needs to be a DBA's ally, not enemy. It is important for a DBA to develop and maintain good relationships with their own manager, and with any other managers in the organization that they work with. Getting along with your own manager makes it easier for you to get the resources you need to succeed at your job. The same is true for getting along with other managers, as many of them may control resources that you need in order to perform your tasks successfully.

One way to help maintain and to nurture this relationship is keep your manager, along with other managers you work with, informed of what you are doing, providing regularly updated reports of the status of the various projects you are working on.

Occasionally, you might find that a manager is proving to be an impediment rather than an aid to performing your duties. This can occur if your manager doesn't come from a DBA background. For example, you manager's training and working experience might be in accounting, production, or even development. Their different backgrounds experiences may mean that they do not understand what DBAs do and how important they are to the organization. This can result in some managers making poor choices in regard to the organization's data. For example, a manager may tell you that SQL Server uptime must be 99.999%, not realizing that to achieve such a high uptime your current budget would have to be doubled.

Rather than just complain to anyone who will listen about how "uninformed" your manager is, the DBA needs to take on the responsibility of educating his or her manager on the duties of the DBA, and their importance, and gently explain how and what he or she can do to make the job of the DBA a little easier. In other words, you may need to mentor your manager in all things relating to the organization's data. And if you can subtly get across the message to your manager that if he works with you to help you succeed in protecting the organization's data, that it will also make him look successful too, that would be a great for everyone involved.

Managing People

Many DBAs find themselves in management positions, such as a senior DBA who is in charge of junior DBAs. Some DBAs at large organizations do this full time, while others combine people management with other DBA duties.

Managing SQL Server-based Applications

New DBAs are often surprised to learn that not only are they responsible for managing SQL Server and its databases, but also any applications that access the database. These varies by organization, but in some places the DBA ends up spending more time managing applications than SQL Server itself.

Chapter 3: Specialize (You can't do it all)

Managing Test Environments

In most, larger organizations, DBAs manage test environments that include test SQL Servers and databases, as well as test database applications. The purpose of this is to allow databases and applications (both in-house and third-party) to be tested before new versions of SQL Server (including patches and service packs), operating systems, or applications are rolled out into production.

Monitoring

This is a wide-ranging task that includes many subtasks, such as monitoring performance, monitoring server disk space, monitoring logs, ensuring jobs have run successfully, checking for errors, and so on. While there are many third-party tools available to perform these tasks, many DBAs spend a lot of time manually monitoring their servers, because they don't have a budget for such tools, or because they are not familiar with them.

Needs/Requirements Analysis

Whether a DBA is involved in development, or just supports third-party applications, they often perform needs/requirements analysis. This can include talking to users, finding out their needs and requirements, and determining the best way to meet them.

Negotiating Service Level Agreements

In many organizations, DBAs become involved in negotiating Service Level Agreements (SLAs). A SLA is an agreement between the customer (the owner of the business application accessing SQL Server databases) and the service provider (the DBA team managing the databases). This agreement sets out the criteria that define "acceptable service". For example, an SLA could define an acceptable response time for a specific type of transaction, and so on. As part of this negotiating process, the DBA will need to educate the customers and correctly set their expectations with regard to what is and isn't feasible given the resource constraints of the organization.

Performance Tuning

Everyone wants their data right now, not caring about other users. It is the job of the DBA to monitor performance and to determine ways to optimize database performance. This can be a very complex topic, and many DBAs specialize in this area.

Project Management

Oftentimes, DBAs will find themselves in charge of a large project involving many other people. This could entail writing a new in-house application, or managing the migration of a data center from one location to another. DBAs with good project management skills are in high demand.

Protector of the Data

While this is not a specific job task, I am including it here because it underlies so many of the DBA's other tasks. DBAs are responsible for protecting the integrity of an organization's data. This not only involves such obvious areas as back and restore and high availability, it also includes ensuring that applications don't corrupt data, that hardware doesn't corrupt data, or that user's don't corrupt data.

Replicating Data

It is very common for data to be moved from one server to another on a regular basis. For example, data from a SQL Server instance in one city needs to be moved to another SQL Server instance in another city. A DBA will often research various ways in which data can be replicated from server to server, decide upon the most appropriate method, implement the replication, and then manage it once it is up and running.

Report Writing

With the advent of SQL Server Reporting Services, many DBAs find themselves writing reports against databases. This might just mean writing the Transact-SQL code to extract the data, or it could include the creation and formatting of physical reports. This is a new and growing area, and some DBAs are becoming specialists in it.

Chapter 3: Specialize (You can't do it all)

Running Jobs

Virtually every SQL Server has jobs that run on it periodically. These jobs might include backups, data imports or exports, or rebuilding indexes. DBAs are responsible for determining what jobs are needed, creating the jobs, and managing them.

Security

DBAs control who can access data and what they can do with it. This involves creating SQL Server login IDs, database IDs, assigning permissions, moving security between servers, and maybe even implementing data encryption.

Scripting

DBAs often write their own Transact-SQL scripts to perform a wide range of tasks, including monitoring and maintenance tasks. In addition, with the advent of PowerShell, many DBAs are writing PowerShell scripts to enhance their productivity.

SSIS/ETL

A very common task is to move data in and out of databases and at the same time perform some transformations on the data as it is moved. This is often done for BI applications, data warehouses, and application integration. SQL Server Integration Services (SSIS) is a popular tool DBAs use to implement Export/Transform/Load (ETL) operations in SQL Server.

Testing

DBAS perform all sorts of testing, all the time. This can include testing servers, testing databases, testing applications, testing management tools, and so on. DBAs test because they want to ensure that what they do will work, and that data integrity and high availability, is maintained at all times.

Chapter 3: Specialize (You can't do it all)

Training Users

Oftentimes, DBAs need to share their knowledge with other DBAs, developers, or end-users. This might be informal one-on-one tutoring, or it might include classroom training.

Troubleshooting

Virtually every day, DBAs are troubleshooting one problem or another. In many cases, when a problem occurs the DBA is expected to "drop everything" and focus on resolving the problem at hand.

Vendor Relations

Many SQL Server-based applications are provided by third-parties, so the DBA often becomes involved with maintaining relationships with these third-party vendors. The DBA will generally perform the initial installation of the third-party software, troubleshoot problems, and update the application and its database when new versions are rolled out.

Working with Teammates

Rarely will a DBA work alone. In most cases, DBAs will be interacting with a very large group of people, including other DBAs, developers, end-users, product-knowledge specialists, vendors, accountants, hardware experts, and networking experts.

Choosing a Specialty

As you can see, DBAs perform many different functions. While you may find specialist DBAs who focus in particular areas, it is rare to find a DBA that performs all of the tasks listed above.

The reason it is rare to find a DBA who can perform every type of DBA function is because it requires knowing way more than you can expect of most people. There is also the added burden of having to keep up with each technology as it changes. For most people, this is impossible. To become an

Chapter 3: Specialize (You can't do it all)

Exceptional DBA, you don't have to know everything there is about SQL Server. In fact, you have a much better chance of becoming an Exceptional DBA if you narrow your focus and specialize in a single area of SQL Server.

When I recommend that you pick a DBA specialty, I don't mean that you only focus on your specialty to the exclusion of all other DBA functions. It is still important for a DBA, especially for the Exceptional DBA, to be familiar with other DBA areas. This rounded knowledge base helps the DBA be aware of other areas that may directly impact his or her specialty.

In the following sections, I describe some of the more common "specialist areas" as a guide to get you thinking about the options available to you.

DBA System Administrator

The DBA System Administrator is a generalist, needing an extensive knowledge of many different areas. Also known as a Production DBA, the DBA System Administrator is generally in charge of setting up, configuring, and maintaining test and production SQL Server instances. This can include such routine tasks as monitoring, tuning, backups and restores, security, creating jobs, and so on. In medical terms, think of the DBA System Administrator as a General Practice doctor. All of the other DBA specialties are more like the medical specialists, such as a surgeon or dermatologist.

DBA Database Designer

The DBA Database Designer focuses on creating new database schemas. He defines user needs and requirements, develops logical database designs, creates physical databases, and so on. In most cases, the DBA Database Designer will work with DBA Developers, or other developers, to help develop or maintain applications.

DBA Developer

The DBA Developer writes code, be that Transact-SQL scripts, stored procedures, functions, CLR objects, or any other kind of code that is used to access SQL Server data. Often, the DBA Developer will work with DBA

Chapter 3: Specialize (You can't do it all)

System Administrators, DBA Database Designers, Project Managers, and other developers to develop and maintain applications.

DBA High Availability Specialist

For many organizations, it is critical that SQL Server is available "around the clock". Therefore, there has become a need for DBAs who specialize in high availability. Their job is to determine what high availability methods are best for their environment, and then to implement and maintain them.

DBA Business Intelligence Specialist

DBA Business Intelligence Specialists design, create, and maintain data warehouses and OLAP cubes so that data can more easily be retrieved and analyzed by organizations. This often involves developing BI-based applications, written using MDX queries. They also design or configure Business Intelligence tools for use by end-users.

DBA Report Writer

In the past, the DBA Report Writer has often been lumped with the Business Intelligence Specialist. However, SQL Server Reporting Services has evolved enough now that many DBAs are needed just to design and create reports in order to extract data from databases in meaningful ways.

Chapter 3: Specialize (You can't do it all)

Summary: Specialize but be Adaptable

Given that the DBA job description is so varied, and constantly changing, it is hard to list all the possible DBA specialties on which you might want to focus, so don't consider the above lists to be anything more than a guide.

You may find that you want to develop your own specialty, one that is even more focused than the broad specializations I've described in this chapter. For example, maybe you want to focus on performance tuning, clustering, SSIS, or replication. There is nothing preventing you from specializing as much as you like, other than the fact that the more narrow your specialty, the less jobs you will find.

While I highly suggest you select a specialty and become very good at it, I want to end this chapter with two thoughts about specialization. First, business needs change. In other words, over time the demand for DBA specialties changes. Therefore, you may need to periodically review your specialty to determine whether or not there is still a strong market need for it. If the need for your specialty is declining, then you will need to move to a different one. For example, how many people today still earn a living writing dBase applications?

Second, over time, your interests may change. You may decide that, after specializing in one particular area for five years, you need a "change of scenery". Very few people are interested in staying in the exact same job for their entire career. Don't be afraid to change specialties when the time is right.

Chapter 4: Hone Your Skill Set

Chapter 3 took an "A-to-Z" tour of typical technical tasks that the DBA might be expected to undertake. However, becoming an Exceptional DBA involves many skills, not just mastering the technical aspects of SQL Server.

In this chapter, we examine the various ingredients that will help you establish a career as a DBA and then contribute to your long-term success as an Exceptional DBA. These ingredients include:

- **Formal Education** – you don't need a degree in database administration, but a solid computer technology background will help.
- **Getting Experience** – getting experience as a new DBA can be tough, but it can be done.
- **Technical skills** – sound knowledge of SQL Server is not enough on its own; the DBA needs to understand the underlying operating system and hardware, as well as the productivity tools that are available to them.
- **Soft Skills** – the DBA needs to supplement sound technical skills with excellent teamwork, time management, writing skills, and more.

Where Does Formal Education Fit In?

I frequently get asked whether or not you need a formal degree to become a DBA. While having a formal degree is not mandatory for becoming an Exceptional DBA, it is a great start.

Chapter 4: Hone Your Skill Set

Higher Education

Very few universities offer an Associates, Bachelors, Masters or PhD degrees in database administration. I believe the reason for the lack of database administration degrees in most schools is twofold. First, the market for database administrators is smaller than most other educational markets. Second, very few people come out of high (secondary) school wanting to become a database administrator. In a perfect world, a degree in database administration would be an ideal platform from which to embark on a DBA career. The reality is that there are few of these educational opportunities available.

Therefore, the most common approach people take to prepare for a career as a database administrator (either through foresight or dumb luck) is to get a degree in Computer Science (CS) or Information Technology (IT), which includes database-specific courses. In fact, when many people attend a university to attain one of these degrees, they are not aware that the career of DBA even exists, and first discover databases when taking database theory classes as part of their degree program. Such a degree provides a rounded education in computer technology and provides a great foundation for becoming a DBA.

The reality is that most people don't go to college to become a database administrator, or even to work in the technology field, so they get Bachelor's degrees in other subjects, ranging anywhere from English to Business, or from Art to Math. It is only when they enter the workforce and experience the real world that they realize they are interested in computer technology, or in becoming a database professional.

Many people wind up as database administrators through a set of often-random circumstances. In fact, many DBAs don't have degrees in computer technology, and I am one of them. I have a Bachelors degree in both Economics and Business Administration, and a Masters Degree in Business Administration.

While a bachelors degree in a non-computer technology field may not be as ideal a foundation as having a degree in a computer technology, it can still provide a rounded education that people can leverage to reach whatever goals that interest them. My degrees in Economics and Business Administration actually helped my computer career a lot. As I had a good understanding of

Chapter 4: Hone Your Skill Set

accounting and how businesses worked, I was much better equipped to work in the real world than most newly minted programmers.

The main point I want to make is that, while a computer technology-related degree may be the best preparation for a DBA career, don't be discouraged if you have a different degree. For example, I know successful DBA who have degrees in:

Clinical Psychology

Creative Writing

Geology

Engineering

Organizational Psychology

Pharmacy

Philosophy

Hydrology

Linguistics

Business Administration

Music

Divinity Studies

Finance

Economics

Chemistry

Political Science

Accounting

Tropical Forestry

Physics

Actuarial Science

Whatever your educational background, use the skills you developed earning your degree, be prepared to teach yourself the skills you need, and look out for opportunities.

During my degree, I learned BASIC, and later taught some BASIC programming classes at a local community college. My first IT job after graduation was as a computer salesperson and trainer (an odd combination indeed) at one of the first computer stores opened in the United States. I got the job because I owned an IBM PC, which was a rare tool for most people to own at that time, and because of my teaching experience. After that, I began writing about computer technology, and then moved through a wide range of computer-related jobs, ranging from application development, software support, network administration, and full-time trainer, before finally arriving at database administrator.

Employer Expectations

Now, let's talk a little about what employers expect when it comes to formal education. Whether you agree or not, a Bachelors degree is becoming the minimum educational credential for most professional jobs. Many companies won't even consider someone for a job unless they have at least four years of higher education. It's a fine line though: a two-year degree is generally not considered an adequate substitute for a four-year degree, but a Masters or PhD degree can often make a person seem to be over-educated for many jobs (unless the job specifically requires a Masters or PhD degree as the minimum educational requirement). This makes the standard four-year Bachelors degree the best route for most people. I only got my Masters degree because I wanted to be able to teach at the college level, and this requires a Masters degree at the very minimum.

If you look at job-wanted ads for database professionals, you will find that most employers want someone who has a four-year computer technology degree, or equivalent. In other words, they prefer someone who has a computer technology education, but many are willing to accept someone with any four-year degree if they meet the other skills and experience required by the position. If you are starting out in your career, and want to become a database professional, the more closely aligned your education is to computer technology, the easier it will be to find jobs.

How about those people who don't have a four-year degree? Is it possible for them to become database professionals? Yes, but it is tougher. I know DBAs who have not attended a university, or perhaps attended for a while, but never attained a degree. These people often start with companies in a low-level computer technology job, such as working the help desk. Then, through self-study, on-the-job training, experience, or by accident, they eventually move into the DBA role.

Most of these individuals stay with a single company as they develop their skills. Once they have developed a lot of experience as a DBA, they can move to other companies, who are willing to waive the four-year degree minimum requirement in return for the hands-on experience that they offer. Of course, some companies won't waive this requirement, and so certain job opportunities will remain closed to non-degree candidates.

Switching Careers

Up until this point, we have been considering formal university training at the beginning of one's career. What if you already have an IT career, but want to switch to become a database professional? For example, maybe you are a developer who wants to stop writing code and focus on database administration. How does formal education fit into this scenario? If you already have a computer technology-related degree, you are in good shape. All you need to do is gain specific database-related skills and experience. If you have a non-technology-related degree, and you have lots of technology experience (say you have been a network administrator for three years or more), you are also in good shape for making the transition, if you attain the necessary DBA skills.

If you don't have a technology-related degree, or technology-related work experience, then changing careers to become a database professional is more problematic. In this regard, it is as if you are starting from scratch. You might want to consider going back to school (part- or full-time) to get a degree in computer technology or database administration (where available). If you already have a degree, getting a second degree should be much faster.

Getting Experience

While a good and relevant formal education is an excellent first step to becoming an Exceptional DBA, it is just a start. Universities generally only cover database theory, not specific database skills. Even if you were to graduate from a university with a Masters or PhD degree in database administration, you won't be prepared for the day-to-day work as a DBA. Learning the practical side of being a DBA takes additional technical knowledge and a lot of practical experience.

In almost every job ad you see for a DBA, experience is required. So how do you get your first job as a DBA if you don't have any experience as a DBA, and how can you get experience as a DBA if you can't get a job as a DBA in the first place? Most new job seekers face this same dilemma, especially if they are looking for professional-caliber jobs. So what do you do?

One option is to apply for DBA jobs that don't require experience. If you have training as a DBA, and have a degree or certification to verify your credentials, some companies will hire you. DBAs are in such high demand now that some companies hire DBAs without experience. If the company is large, they may even offer a training program to get you started out right.

However, the fact remains that most people who become new DBAs are promoted to that position from another position within the company they currently work for. In other words, they have been working for a company for some time in some computer-related position, have a good track record, and have expressed an interest in becoming a DBA. Oftentimes, if a company cannot find an experienced DBA to fill a position, they will recruit from within, and train the person for the job.

What if you are working for a company that doesn't have a DBA position open? Or maybe the company is too small to need a full-time DBA. What do you do then? One option would be to identify any DBA-type work done within your current company and volunteer to do it as part of your regular job. This will start getting you hands-on DBA experience, even if it is only on a part-time basis. If your current job does not afford you the opportunity to gain any DBA experience, you may have to consider changing jobs, and finding a company where DBA opportunities exist. It is either this option, or trying to find a job that will hire a DBA without experience.

Chapter 4: Hone Your Skill Set

What if you can't change jobs right now, and don't have any opportunities to get any practical DBA experience? At this point, you are running out of options. You might contact non-profit organizations and volunteer your services, or you might attend a local SQL Server user's group and ask the members for their suggestions on how you can get experience in your local area. Attending SQL Server user groups offer many benefits both when learning new skills, and when looking for a job. You will get the opportunity to network with fellow DBAs, and new jobs are often announced to the group. Furthermore, attendees may get the opportunity to announce to the group they are looking for new DBA work and, oftentimes, recruiters show up looking for new talent.

However you gain your DBA experience, you will find that it is the most important asset you can have.

Mastering DBA Technical Skills

Once you have embarked on your new career as a DBA, you need to quickly master the practical technical skills that will allow you to succeed in the job. In this section, we take a broad look at the specific kinds of technical skills you need to become an Exceptional DBA, along with suggestions on how to attain them.

Specialized Database Skills

As we discussed in Chapter 2, it is virtually impossible for anyone to know everything there is to know about databases. Because of this, I suggested that you specialize in an area that interests you. This might be DBA System Administration, DBA Database Designer, DBA Development, DBA Business Intelligence, among others.

The key to becoming an Exceptional DBA is to select a specialty, and then master all the technical information related to it. For example, if you want to become a DBA System Administrator, you need to learn about how the database engine works, how to perform routine maintenance tasks, how to performance tune, how to troubleshoot problems, and so on. Pick whatever DBA specialty interests you, and make it a point to master it, inside and out. If you don't know what specialty to pick, I recommend you start as a DBA

System Administrator. As you begin to master these skills, you will also be learning about the other specialties, and you can always change specialties anytime you want.

Hardware

Not only is the Exceptional DBA an expert in their chosen SQL Server specialty, they are also very knowledgeable about the physical computer hardware on which SQL Server runs. Getting the best performance and scalability out of SQL Server requires DBAs to know how to select the optimum hardware for their SQL Server. In addition, hardware skills are necessary for knowing how to best configure the hardware, along with how to diagnose and troubleshoot hardware-related problems. Exceptional DBAs don't depend on others to figure out problems with their servers.

Operating System

Another critical component the Exceptional DBA needs to understand is the operating system. It is fully intertwined with SQL Server and the physical hardware, and can't be separated. The DBA needs to know how to install it, configure it, manage it, and troubleshoot it. Many problems that are associated with SQL Server are operating-system related, and the Exceptional DBA needs to understand its intricacies in order to resolve them.

Productivity Tools

Whatever database specialty you choose, you will have both built-in and third-party tools available to help you do your job and be more productive. In my experience, many DBAs don't take the time to learn how to master the tools available to them. This means they end up being less proficient and productive at their work.

Not only does the Exceptional DBA master all the tools included with SQL Server, he also learns about related third-party tools that can help him become more productive. This means they often are downloading new tools, and trying them out, seeing if they help them become more productive.

Chapter 4: Hone Your Skill Set

SQL Server Best Practices

In addition to the raw technical knowledge that a DBA requires, there is an additional layer of knowledge that Exceptional DBAs must gain, and that is SQL Server Best Practices. As a DBA, you are often many faced with many different ways to perform the same task. Some of the options are better than others, especially if you factor in the requirements of a specific situation. Best Practices refers to the best way to perform a specific task, given the circumstances you are facing. For example, there are different ways to back up and restore databases, and the best way to do this often depends on the situation.

Unfortunately, most SQL Server Best Practices have not been codified. Instead, you have to search them out from books, articles, and websites. In other cases, you have to learn them by trial and error. The Exceptional DBA often develops his or her own set of Best Practices and uses them in their day to day work, helping them not only to bring consistency to their work, but also to help them perform their job better and more efficiently.

How to Obtain DBA Technical Skills

As you can see, Exceptional DBAs need to have a wide variety of technical skills. So how do they attain them? It really comes down to making time to do so; both time for learning and time for gaining experience. As discussed earlier, a DBA needs many technical skills that won't generally be taught at a university. Instead, most Exceptional DBAs master technical skills by using one or more of the methods detailed below.

An Exceptional DBA will probably use most of these training methods at one time or another. You may find that some are better suited to you than others. It really doesn't make much difference which option you choose, as long as you take the time to learn. Mastering the technical skills to become an Exceptional DBA is your responsibility. In other words, you have to design your own education program. Nobody is going to do it for you. Yes, you can get some help by taking a series of related courses, such as certification courses (see Chapter 5), but that is just a beginning. You need to decide what skills you need to meet the knowledge requirements of your chosen DBA specialty, and to decide how you are going to acquire those skills.

Chapter 4: Hone Your Skill Set

Formal Classroom Training

Formal classroom training is offered by corporate training companies, and some colleges and universities (usually non-credit), and is one of the fastest ways to master multiple technical skills, including SQL Server, hardware, and the operating system. Many of these classes are called "certification classes" because the assumption is that once you take the class, you should be ready to take the related certification test, assuming you want to become certified. While these can be expensive, they are an effective way to learn a lot of information very quickly, especially if the subject matter is new to you.

Seminars and Workshops

These are training sessions that last one day or two and focus on a very specific topic. Generally speaking, these are best for people who already have some background in the subject matter and are looking for more in-depth knowledge of a particular subject.

Conferences

Conferences encompass many different learning formats, including formal classroom training, half-day and one-day workshops, short (60-90 minute) seminars, hands-on training labs, and general sessions. Most even offer opportunities to ask database experts specific questions about any topic you want to learn more about, on a one-on-one basis. If you are a new DBA, conferences can be a little overwhelming, but educational. In many cases, you will see experienced DBAs attending conferences not only to learn something new, but to network and make new connections.

User Group Meetings

User groups are another source of learning. Not only can you learn from local and national speakers, you get the opportunity to ask questions of speakers and other attendees, mining their knowledge for solutions to your problems. User group meetings are also a good place to network.

Chapter 4: Hone Your Skill Set

On-line Training

Learning over the Internet is becoming more and more common, but the cost and the quality of the learning varies substantially. In some cases, you can take free lessons that range from average to exceptional in quality, and in other cases you can pay a lot of money for mediocre to exceptional training. If you intend to pay a lot of money for on-line training, be sure you carefully check out the company first before you send them your money.

Self-Study Booking Learning

One of the most popular ways to master SQL Server technical skills is to read books. There are books on virtually every topic and at most every learning level. Books allow you to choose when you learn, but on the other hand, you have to be disciplined enough to take book learning seriously if you want to get the most out of your time.

Magazines and other Publications

There are few technical magazines or publications that focus on SQL Server, or databases for that matter. Of those that are available, they are most useful for keeping up with SQL Server news and third-party products, but they are not always the best way to learn new skills.

Websites, Blogs, News, RSS Feeds

By contrast, there are many different websites and blogs devoted to SQL Server. Unfortunately, the quality of the content varies widely, and much of it can be out of date. This means that you may have to spend a little extra time searching for SQL Server-related websites and articles that cover the specific material you want to master. Many DBAs consider this type of learning as "just-in-time" learning. In other words, if you need to learn a specific skill or task very quickly, then the Internet is often the quickest way to find the content and to learn it.

Chapter 4: Hone Your Skill Set

On the Job Training Opportunities

If you work for a larger organization, they may offer on-the-job learning opportunities, including formal instruction and mentoring. If you have these options are available, you will want to take advantage of them.

Mastering DBA Soft Skills

If you want to become an Exceptional DBA, not only do you need exceptional technical skills, you also need to master many soft skills. Yes, I know what you are thinking. You are thinking that if you are a technical wiz, you don't need soft skills. Unfortunately, that's not the case. As we discussed earlier in the book, Exceptional DBAs have many traits that fall into the soft skills category.

The following sections describe some of the numerous types of soft skills that the Exceptional DBA should master.

People Skills

While this phrase may be overused, it is overused with much justification. While DBAs may find themselves working alone more than some professionals do, they still need to work with others. This includes talking with end-users, developers, vendors, IT professionals, and managers. If you don't get along well with others, you will severely reduce your chances of becoming an Exceptional DBA, or even of having a long career as a DBA.

If you don't naturally have people skills, learning them can be difficult, but you do have some options available to you. You might consider reading books on people skills, taking classes or seminars, or even individual counseling. While people skills may be hard to learn, learning them will pay off for your entire life.

Chapter 4: Hone Your Skill Set

Teamwork Skills

I consider teamwork skills to be a little different than people skills, although there is a lot of overlap. People skills are about getting along well with others. Teamwork skills are about learning how to work well with others. Many times, you find yourself in a team of people that you did not pick, and would not pick if you had a choice. Teamwork skills are learning how to work effectively in a team and get things done, even if you don't like each other!

As a part of a team, you might be the leader (also requiring leadership and project management skills), or you may be a contributor who is assigned a task that needs to be completed. Whatever role you fall in, you need to participate and work together as a team to accomplish the task successfully and on schedule.

If you have difficulty with teamwork skills, you may first want to work on your people skills. Once you have accomplished this, then focus on building teamwork skills. There are many books and seminars available on building and managing teams. In fact, your organization might even offer one in-house. If so, jump at the first opportunity at taking it.

Personal Time Management Skills

Most Exceptional DBAs have more work than they have time to accomplish. To get everything done, the DBA needs to be effective at managing his of her time. It is very easy to just sit back and have work come to you, pile up, with much of it never getting done. Instead, you must be proactive when managing your time. Keep a schedule and assign priorities to tasks so you can ensure that what has to get done gets done, on time, and successfully. Don't be afraid to say "no" to new tasks if you don't have the time to do them right in the first place.

If you have trouble managing your own time, start small by using a schedule, making appointments for yourself to ensure work gets done. Using Microsoft Outlook, or a similar tool, is a great way to track tasks, appointments, meetings, and other things you need to accomplish. If this doesn't work for you, there are many books and seminars available on personal time management.

Project Management

If you want to be an Exceptional DBA, you will find yourself managing many projects, from the smallest that take a single day and just yourself to complete, to those that take a year and many people to complete. Project Management is like personal time management, but on a much larger scale. Depending on the complexity of the project, you may spend all of your time managing it instead of actually producing any work yourself.

Project management is a skill set most people don't naturally possess. It has to be learned through training and experience. It is much more than just learning how to use Microsoft Project and creating nice-looking PERT charts. It involves managing people and other resources, over time, to accomplish a specific goal. While you can buy books about project management, the best way to learn it is by taking formal classes or seminars on it. Once you have learned the basics, then it is usually trial by fire when you begin your first project. Hopefully, it will be a small project that will give you the experience you need before tackling large projects.

Leadership Skills

Leadership is a hard concept to define. Essentially, it is the ability to define an objective, to clearly communicate what the objective is and why it is important, and then to get other people to help you reach that objective.

When many people think about leadership, they think about politicians or corporate CEOs. While they need to have good leadership skills, so does the Exceptional DBA. In many cases, the ability to be able to clearly define goals, communicate them to others, and then to get others to work toward the common goal, is a valuable skill. Leadership can come into play in meetings, teams, or large projects. You don't have to be a manager to be a leader.

Most people don't consider themselves leadership material. However, in many cases they are doing themselves an injustice. Everyone has the ability to define goals, communicate them, and get other people to help attain them. Essentially, it is a matter of planning and execution, sprinkled with a lot of people skills. While you can take leadership classes, the best way to learn leadership skills is to take on the responsibilities of a leader, and get hands-on experience.

Chapter 4: Hone Your Skill Set

Writing Skills

As much as you might dislike writing, it is a very important skill to learn. Virtually every day you will find yourself communicating with others in writing, whether it's via an e-mail, some documentation, or a formal report. Unfortunately, writing is a skill that is poorly taught by most schools, including universities. If you realize you don't have the skills to be a good writer (grammar, punctuation, style), then you need to take it upon yourself to learn these. This is not easy, especially if your previous schooling has been weak. Your best option is to take formal writing classes to master these skills. While you can read books and take short seminars on writing, it is hard to learn how to write well unless you get regular feedback.

Once you have learned writing basics, the next step is to develop your skill by practicing. The more you write, the better you will become. Many DBAs who want to become better writers get experience by writing articles for websites and magazines. As a beginner, you may not get paid much, or not at all. Nevertheless, and more importantly, you will get the experience and feedback that will help make you a better writer, a better communicator, and a better DBA.

Speaking Skills

We have all heard that public speaking is the most feared of all human activities. I am not sure that I fully agree with this statement, but public speaking does not come naturally to many people. Learning public speaking skills is important for the Exceptional DBA because you will find yourself doing it, whether you plan to or not. For example, you may have to present at a business meeting, teach an in-house seminar, or even find yourself talking at a user group meeting. What most people don't realize about speaking is that you have to plan it, you just can't wing it.

Like writing, I feel that the best way to learn public speaking is by taking formal training classes and/or seminars. You might also want to join a speaking club, such as Toastmasters International. Once you have the fundamentals down, then you need to practice and practice. Start small and work yourself up to speaking to larger and larger groups, and from short sessions to longer sessions.

Chapter 4: Hone Your Skill Set

Knowledge of Legal Responsibilities

As DBAs, we often find ourselves involved in fulfilling legal responsibilities, such as maintaining data privacy, or archiving data for legally defined periods of time. In order to carry out the legal responsibilities of the job, you have to know what your responsibilities are. Simply claiming to be ignorant of the law won't work. In fact, it is possible to go to jail for failing to meet legal obligations.

The difficulty is in finding out what those legal responsibilities are, as they vary from industry to industry, state to state, and country to country. Because you are not an attorney, and because your manager is not an attorney, it is important that you ask the upper management of your organization to specifically define what your legal responsibilities are, along with how to best implement them.

Summary: Starting Honing Your Skills Today (and don't stop)

Becoming an Exceptional DBA involves more than just knowing a lot about SQL Server. It includes knowing about hardware, the operating system, best practices, leadership, time management, communication skills, and much more. This may seem like a lot of material to master. And it is. Nobody can be expected to master all of this in a short time period. Instead, it is accomplished over time.

If you find that you come up short in some of these critical knowledge areas, start today by picking out one or two of them and then work on them every day until you master them. Only through perseverance and hard work will you become an Exceptional DBA.

CHAPTER 5: IS PROFESSIONAL CERTIFICATION NECESSARY?

Bring up the merits of professional certification with a group of DBAs, and you are guaranteed to start an argument. Some DBAs are proud of their certifications and maintain them assiduously, taking new exams as each new version of the software is released, and displaying all their certificates above their desk. Others are certified, but don't publicize the fact. Some DBAs get certified at the start of their career, but then don't bother renewing their certification when new products are released. And there are yet other DBAs who brag about the fact that they have never taken a certification exam, nor will they ever take one.

According to Microsoft, as of April 2009:

- 153,130 people have received the MCDBA: SQL Server 2000 certification
- 51,445 people have received the MCTS: SQL Server 2005 certification
- 854 people have received the MCTS: SQL Server 2008 Implementation and Maintenance certification
- 3,577 people have received the MCTS: SQL Server 2005 Business Intelligence certification
- 333 people have received the MCTS: SQL Server 2008 Business Intelligence Development and Maintenance certification
- 456 people have received the MCTS: SQL Server 2008 Database Development certification
- 7,928 people have received the MCITP: SQL Server 2005 Database Administrator certification
- 358 people have received the MCITP: SQL Server 2008 Database Administrator certification
- 3,377 people have received the MCITP: SQL Server 2005 Database Developer certification
- 213 people have received the MCITP: SQL Server 2008 Database Developer certification
- 1,385 people have received the MCITP: SQL Server 2005 Business Intelligence Developer certification

Chapter 5: Is Professional Certification Necessary?

- 137 people have received the MCITP: SQL Server 2008 Business Intelligence Developer certification
- 18 people have received the MCA: Database certification
- 39 people have received the MCM: SQL Server 2005 certification
- 2 people have received the MCM: SQL Server 2008 certification

As you can see, while the SQL Server 2000 MCDBA certification was very popular, the newer SQL Server 2005 and SQL Server 2008 certifications have been much less so. While it is hard to know the reason for this, it might be an indication that certification is not as important to DBAs as it has been in the past.

When it really comes down to it, becoming certified in SQL Server does not make you an Exceptional DBA. In fact, many Exceptional DBAs have never taken a certification test. However, in my opinion, there are definite advantages to certification, depending on your situation. In this chapter, we will examine the different types of certification available, and some of the benefits of certification. We will finish the chapter by trying to answer that age-old question: "Should I get certified as a DBA?"

SQL Server Certification

Over the years, Microsoft has offered a wide range of different certifications for SQL Server. Certifications first became available with SQL Server 6.5, with separate tests for administration and development. SQL Server 7.0 followed the same format. When SQL Server 2000 was introduced, certification was changed to the MCDBA, which required 4 exams to achieve certification. With the introduction of SQL Server 2005, Microsoft introduced two different types of SQL Server certifications: the Microsoft Certified Technology Specialist (MCTS) and Microsoft Certified IT Professional (MCITP). For SQL Server 2008, Microsoft continues to offer the MCTS and MCITP certifications, with some minor changes. We will talk about each of these certifications in the next section.

NOTE:
I won't discuss the Microsoft Certified Master: SQL Server 2008 certification, which is out of the financial reach of nearly everyone. If you

Chapter 5: Is Professional Certification Necessary?

want to find out more about it, visit: www.microsoft.com/learning/mcp/master/sql/default.mspx

As you may guess, Microsoft is recommending that you skip the SQL Server 2005 certifications and get certified in SQL Server 2008 instead. I concur with this, as the latest credential is almost always the most beneficial. For the latest certification news, check out Microsoft's learning portal at: www.microsoft.com/learning/mcp/default.mspx

Microsoft Certified Technology Specialist

The Microsoft Certified Technology Specialist (MCTS) certification is designed to recognize an individual's skills in a specific Microsoft technology. Microsoft offers a wide variety of Technology Specialist certifications, including two that are of specific interest to DBAs of SQL Server 2005, and three that are of specific interest to DBAs of SQL Server 2008.

The SQL Server 2005 MCTS certification includes these two options:

- SQL Server 2005 Technology Specialist
- SQL Server 2005 Business Intelligence Technology Specialist

To receive the SQL Server 2005 Technology Specialist credential, you must pass the exam: Microsoft SQL Server 2005 – Implementation and Maintenance (70-431). This exam tests your knowledge of SQL Server 2005 tools usage, tool navigation, wizard use, Transact-SQL, code debugging, and troubleshooting. It is designed for all DBAs, and is the most basic of all the SQL Server 2005 tests available. It encompasses the foundation of knowledge that all SQL Server DBAs should possess.

To receive the SQL Server 2005 Business Intelligence Technology Specialist credential, you must pass the exam: Microsoft SQL Server 2005 Business Intelligence—Implementation and Maintenance (70-445). This exam tests your knowledge of SQL Server 2005 SSAS management, SSAS development, data mining, managing SSRS, report development, BI solutions development, and SSIS administration. It is designed for DBAs who specialize in SQL Server 2005 business intelligence, and encompasses the foundation of knowledge that all SQL Server Business Intelligence DBAs should possess.

Chapter 5: Is Professional Certification Necessary?

The SQL Server 2008 MCTS certification includes these three options (one more than with SQL Server 2005):

- SQL Server 2008 Implementation and Maintenance
- SQL Server 2008 Database Development
- SQL Server 2008 Business Intelligence Development and Maintenance

To receive the SQL Server 2008 Implementation and Maintenance Specialist credential, you must pass the exam 70-432, which covers the following topics: installing and configuring, maintaining SQL instances, managing security, managing a database, data management tasks, monitoring and troubleshooting, optimizing, and implementing high availability.

To receive the SQL Server 2008 Database Development credential, you must pass the exam 70-433, which covers Transact-SQL coding and development.

To receive the SQL Server 2008 Business Intelligence Development and Maintenance credential, you must pass the exam 70-448, which covers the following topics: configuring, deploying, maintaining and implementing SSIS, SSRS, and SSAS.

To receive any of the above certifications, only a single test is required. A side benefit of taking any of the above exams is that they get you one-step closer to receiving the Microsoft Certified IT Professional certification, as each of these exams counts towards this certification.

Microsoft Certified IT Professional

The Microsoft Certified IT Professional (MCITP) certification is Microsoft's premier certification. It encompasses multiple tests, each of which covers a specific subject matter area. Microsoft offers three different IT Professional certifications of interest to DBAs, for both SQL Server 2005 and SQL Server 2008:

- Database Administrator
- Database Developer
- Business Intelligence Developer

Chapter 5: Is Professional Certification Necessary?

The MCITP certification includes multiple tests (different tests for SQL Server 2005 and 2008) and covers a wider range of subject matter knowledge, so this certification is considered superior than the Technology Specialists certifications.

Database Administrator IT Professional

As its name indicates, this certification is designed for DBA Administrators, and includes three required exams for SQL Server 2005:

- Microsoft SQL Server 2005 – Implementation and Maintenance (70-431)
- Designing a Database Server Infrastructure by Using Microsoft SQL Server 2005 (70-443)
- Optimizing and Maintaining a Database Administration Solution by Using Microsoft SQL Server 2005 (70-444)

For SQL Server 2008, only two exams, not three, are required to receive your Database Administrator MCITP:

- Microsoft SQL Server 2008, Installation and Maintenance (70-432)
- Designing, Optimizing and Maintaining a Database Server Infrastructure using Microsoft SQL Server 2008 (70-450)

Database Developer IT Professional

This certification is designed for DBAs who focus on database development, and includes three required exams for SQL Server 2005.

- Microsoft SQL Server 2005 – Implementation and Maintenance (70-431)
- Designing Database Solutions by Using Microsoft SQL Server 2005 (70-441)
- Designing and Optimizing Data Access by Using Microsoft SQL Server 2005 (70-442)

For SQL Server 2008, only two exams, not three, are required to receive your Database Developer MCITP:

- Microsoft SQL Server 2008, Database Development (70-433)
- Designing Database Solutions and Data Access Using Microsoft SQL Server 2008 (70-451)

Chapter 5: Is Professional Certification Necessary?

Business Intelligence Developer IT Professional

This certification is designed for DBAs who specialize in Business Intelligence, and includes two required exams for SQL Server 2005:

- Microsoft SQL Server 2005 Business Intelligence – Implementation and Maintenance (70-445)
- Designing a Business Intelligence Infrastructure by Using Microsoft SQL Server 2005 (70-446)
- For SQL Server 2008, only two exams are required to receive your Business Intelligence Developer MCITP:
- Microsoft SQL Server 2008, Business Intelligence Development and Maintenance (70-448)
- Designing a Business Intelligence Infrastructure Using Microsoft SQL Server 2008 (70-452)

Other Certifications of Interest to DBAs

In the previous chapter, we talked about how important it is for the DBA to be familiar with the hardware and operating system that SQL Server runs on. While you don't have to be certified in hardware or the operating system to be an Exceptional DBA, doing so can certainly help you to round out your knowledge. Below are some certifications that you might consider:

- **CompTIA A+**: Vendor-neutral certification on computer hardware. Recommended for all DBAs so they become familiar with hardware basics.
- **CompTIA Network+**: Vendor-neutral certification on networking. Recommended for all DBAs so they become familiar with networking concepts and troubleshooting.
- **CompTIA Security+**: Vendor-neutral certification on security. You might be interested in this certification if you are a DBA Administrator and have an interest in understanding all aspects of security.
- **Managing & Maintaining a Windows Server 2003 Environment.** This single exam is recommended for all DBAs who work with Windows Server 2003.
- Microsoft Technology Specialist—Windows Server 2008 Network Infrastructure Configuration: If you are running Windows Server 2008, then you may want to consider this exam.

- **Microsoft Certified IT Professional: Server Administrator:** This three exam certification is recommended for all DBA Administrators as it helps provide a deep understanding of the Windows operating system. This is available for Windows Server 2008.
- **Microsoft Certified Professional Developer:** Microsoft offers a variety of certifications for developers. If you are a DBA Developer, attaining one or more of these certifications will help round out your knowledge of how applications interact with SQL Server.

Benefits of Certification

While becoming certified won't make you an Exceptional DBA, I believe it has some key benefits that can contribute to this goal.

Helps to Focus Your Training Efforts

In my opinion, the biggest benefit of becoming certified is that the process of passing exams helps you to focus your learning. In other words, I don't necessarily take exams because I want to have a particular certification; I do it because it forces me to study in a systematic way. Taking and passing exams can act as a motivator to get you to spend the time necessary to master your DBA specialty, and other technology areas important to the DBA.

Broadens your Knowledge

Most of the exams you will take for certification require you to learn a broad range of information and, in that sense; certification exams force you to study technology areas that you might otherwise ignore. For example, let's say that you are a DBA Administrator and focus your learning on administrative tasks. This is great, but if you neglect to learn about how application development affects SQL Server's performance, you are missing out on a lot of useful knowledge.

Distinguishes You from Other DBAs

When it comes time for an internal promotion, or when you are competing for a new job, being certified will help to distinguish you from other candidates. It demonstrates that you keep up with new technology and have mastered the basic skills needed to be a successful DBA.

However, while certification can distinguish you from others, it is not a substitute for experience. In many cases, the more experienced DBA (even without certification) will get the promotion or job over a less experienced DBA with certification.

Some Companies Require Certification

While most companies don't require their DBA to be certified, some do. So, if you are interested in working for a company that only hires certified DBAs, then you have no choice but to become certified.

Company Recognition and Rewards

Some companies treat certified employees differently than non-certified employees. For example, certified employees may be given more responsibility, have better chances of promotion, and may even be paid bonuses based on the certifications they receive.

Peer Recognition

While many DBAs may not care about this, your effort to become certified often brings peer recognition and respect.

Can become a Microsoft Certified Trainer

If you interested in the career opportunities available to a Microsoft Certified Trainer (MCT), you must first get certified in your specialty area. Generally, you will need to get your MCITP before you pursue your MCT credentials.

Chapter 5: Is Professional Certification Necessary?

Potential College Credit

Some colleges and universities will award college credit for taking certification classes and passing certification tests. This can be beneficial if you are finishing your schooling, or are going back to school for additional training, or a new degree.

Microsoft Specific Benefits

Once you pass any Microsoft certification exam, you become a Microsoft Certified Professional (MCP), and Microsoft will offer you some benefits as a reward. Some of these specific benefits include, but are not limited to:

- A listing in the MCP Directory
- Access to a private Microsoft Certification web site, which includes a lot of free information
- Access to the private MCP newsgroups
- Invitations to conferences, training, and special events
- Monthly newsletter subscription
- A transcript that can be printed
- A transcript sharing tool which allows others (prospective employers) to view your transcript
- A printed certificate you can display
- Use of the Microsoft certification logo
- Access to official Microsoft-branded merchandise exclusively for MCPs
- Discount offers for training, exams, publications, and more

Should I Get Certified as a DBA?

As I said earlier, becoming a certified DBA will not make you an Exceptional DBA, and nor does being an Exceptional DBA require that you become a certified DBA. With this in mind, I want to offer the following advice about becoming certified. I offer it with the proviso that everyone is different, so the advice offered here may or may not apply to you. Read my recommendations, and take away from them the advice that best applies to you.

Who Should Seriously Consider Becoming a Certified DBA?

- I highly recommend you get certified as a DBA if you fall into any of the following categories:
- You are currently not a DBA, but want to become a DBA.
- You are a DBA by training or accident, but have little or no practical experience.
- You are a DBA, with or without experience, and you want to work for a company that requires that their DBAs be certified.
- You are a DBA working for a consulting company, and getting certified helps to distinguish yourself and your company from other consulting companies.
- You want to become a Microsoft Certified Trainer and teach SQL Server classes.

Who Should Consider Becoming a Certified DBA?

If you fall into one of the following categories, then I suggest you check out DBA certification, as it may be beneficial to you, although not required.

- You are a DBA and have experience, but your body of knowledge is narrow and you want to broaden that knowledge base.
- For whatever reason, you have not kept up with the latest versions of SQL Server and you want to force yourself to catch up.
- You work in a competitive company and are seeking to become promoted.

Chapter 5: Is Professional Certification Necessary?

- You work in a competitive job market, and you are applying for a new job and you want to distinguish yourself from other job applicants.

Who Might Not Want to Consider Certification?

There are some DBAs who may not be interested in certification, or they may not benefit from being certified.

- You have five or more years of solid DBA experience, and you have no trouble keeping up with the latest in SQL Server technology on your own.
- You are a DBA who was certified in an earlier version of SQL Server, have lots of experience as a DBA, and you have no trouble keeping up with the latest in SQL Server technology, so you don't want to bother being re-certified each time a new version of SQL Server is released.
- You are one of those rare DBAs who don't need any motivation to learn and can do it on your own, and you are so confident in your skills that you don't need to show them off to anyone by becoming certified.

In my experience, DBAs who fall into the latter category tend to be a little arrogant, which is not a good trait for an Exceptional DBA. Having faith in your own ability is fine, but don't let this slip into arrogance or complacency, or you may find it a little harder to find or keep a job as a DBA.

Are There Any Downsides to Certification?

The answer to this depends on what you consider a downside. For example, people might consider the following as downsides to certification, but others will not.

- Taking certification exams costs money.
- Many companies will pay for certification tests for their employees, and if this is the case for you, then this downside is null and void.
- Preparing for certification exams costs money.

If you take a formal class, attend seminars, or even buy books, it will cost you money out of pocket. In fact, if you take formal classes for certification, you can end up spending many thousands of dollars, depending on where you get your training. Again, many companies will pay for certification training as well as for taking the exams. In addition, some U.S. government agencies offer training reimbursement, or you can take advantage of the U.S. federal tax credit for learning, to help offset part of the cost.

Preparing for certification exams takes time.

Many people spend hours of their own time preparing to take certification exams. In other cases, you may work for a company that allows you time off for training, although you will still need to spend some of your personal time on studying. However, even if you don't want to become certified, you will still be spending a lot of your own time studying, in order to keep up with the technology. If you look at it this way, then spending time studying is just part of being a DBA, and is not a downside, unless you don't like to study. And if you don't like to study, then you don't want to become a DBA.

How to Get Your Employer to Help Pay for Your Certification

If you decide you want to go the certification route, and you don't have the financial resources to pay for it yourself, try to enlist the help of your employer. Many employers realize the importance of on-going education and certification, and provide a training budget for their employees. If your company offers such a program, then don't waste this opportunity.

If your employee doesn't have a formal training program, then write up a proposal to your manager, explaining the benefits of you getting trained and certified, along with the associated costs, so the manager knows exactly what is involved. If you write up a thoughtful proposal, demonstrating the benefits for the organization's investment, then you will be on the right track for getting that approval. If your organization isn't interested in helping you out, then you might want to consider finding one that will.

Summary: There is Little Downside to Certification

While you can be an Exceptional DBA without becoming certified, I think that, for most people, there is little to no downside to becoming a certified

Chapter 5: Is Professional Certification Necessary?

DBA. Because of this, I generally recommend certification to those people who ask me about it.

If you are new to SQL Server certification, I suggest you start with the MCTS certification that best matches your SQL Server interests. For example, if you are interested in SQL Server 2008 DBA administration, get the SQL Server 2008 Implementation and Maintenance certification. If you are interested in SQL Server 2008 DBA development, get the SQL Server 2008 Database Development certification, and if you are interested in SQL Server 2008 BI, then get the SQL Server 2008 Business Intelligence Development and Maintenance certification.

Once you have taken one or more of these tests, and you feel ambitious, consider getting the MCITP in your area of specialization. Training and certification is an on-going process, but it can be rewarding if you want to make the most of your career as a DBA.

Chapter 6: Participate in the SQL Server Community

One key trait of the Exceptional DBA is a willingness to share knowledge. This chapter starts by discussing the considerable benefits of sharing your knowledge with the SQL Server community, and then looks in detail at some of the ways in which you can participate.

Benefits of Sharing Your SQL Server Knowledge

Many DBAs regard their job simply as a way to make money. In other words, they use their profession to benefit themselves without any thought to how they could benefit others. I guess there is nothing inherently wrong with this philosophy, but I have discovered that most Exceptional DBAs tend to think a little differently. Instead of just focusing on what their profession can bring to them, they also consider what they can bring to their profession. While at first this might seem contradictory (how can giving of your time help you?), there are many benefits to be gained from sharing your knowledge with the SQL Server community.

Increase Your Depth of Knowledge

Without a doubt, the most common feedback I hear from DBAs who spend a lot of time in SQL Server forums, answering questions, is this: "I have learned more from answering questions than I could learn from any other source." In other words, by giving up some of their own time to help others, they have ended up benefiting enormously from the experience.

How is this possible? Exceptional DBAs use the questions posed in forums as a way to learn more about the behavior of SQL Server. For example, a question posted in a SQL Server forum asks the best way to optimize a particular query. The question includes information on the current table schema, indexes, the data, and the query that is running slowly. An Exceptional DBA will regard such a question as an opportunity to improve

Chapter 6: Participate in the SQL Server Community

their skills. They will consider the question carefully, even doing additional research and testing if necessary, before providing a detailed and thoughtful answer. By repeating the process of reading, analyzing, and answering questions, over and over, the Exceptional DBA will significantly increase the depth of their SQL Server knowledge.

In other cases, Exceptional DBAs will encounter questions that touch areas or behavior that they have never seen before, and that they have no idea how to answer. Again, such questions are often taken as a challenge, and they will research until an answer is found, learning something new about SQL Server in the process. This experience broadens their knowledge base.

While I have used forums as an example of how contributing to the SQL Server community is valuable, this benefit is not limited to forums. For example, every time a DBA writes a blog entry, an article, a book, or makes a presentation to other DBAs, they have an opportunity to learn more about SQL Server from the feedback they receive from their audience.

Virtually every time you participate in the SQL Server community, you will be rewarded with new learning experiences.

Make New Contacts

However you share your knowledge and experience with the SQL Server community, you will be meeting new people. If you participate in forums, you will meet DBAs from all over the world. If you write blog entries, you get to exchange ideas with other DBAs. If you write articles or books, you will attract an audience who enjoys your work, and who often encourage you to write even more.

If you make presentations to local user groups, or national conferences, you get the opportunity not only to meet other DBAs, but also industry leaders and Microsoft SQL Server product team members. These people can provide insight into the industry that you can't get anywhere else. Making new contacts is useful for making new friends, finding new jobs, and learning information to which most people don't have access.

Increase Your Experience and Further Develop Exceptional DBA Traits

Sharing your SQL Server knowledge, and making new friends and contacts, will also help you to develop other essential traits of the Exceptional DBA. For example:

- Writing forum posts, blog entries, articles, and books will help you to develop your written communications skills.
- Making new contacts helps develop your people skills.
- Speaking before groups gives you more experience as an oral communicator.
- Volunteering for local or national user groups helps develop leadership, teamwork, and project management skills.
- Developing your own website helps to develop your writing and coding skills.
- Writing and sharing Transact-SQL scripts helps to develop your Transact-SQL skills.

The examples could go on and on. Almost anything you do to help the SQL Server community will also help to boost your skill set and experience.

It's Fun to Help Others

Another comment I often hear from DBAs who contribute to the SQL Server community is that it is just plain fun to do so. In other words, helping others is fun and makes being a DBA a more enjoyable profession. Whenever you answer a forum question, it's great when the person who asked the question thanks you for your time and effort. When you run a website or write a book, it's a great feeling to receive "fan" mail from people who read and benefitted from what you wrote. Making it into the "top 10 posters" list on a forum, for the month or year, can give you a great sense of achievement.

Along with having fun, helping others can help you gain more self-confidence, which is another important trait of the Exceptional DBA.

Chapter 6: Participate in the SQL Server Community

Become a SQL Server MVP

Microsoft recognizes that DBAs who help other DBAs provide a great benefit to the SQL Server community, besides helping to spread the word about their tools and technology. To help promote and reward community involvement, Microsoft has developed its very successful Most Valuable Professional (MVP) Award program.

Essentially, the MVP Award program recognizes people who are technical and community leaders in their sphere of Microsoft technology (this covers any Microsoft software, not just SQL Server). These are people who are not only subject matter experts, but who also share their technical knowledge with their respective communities. A typical MVP may:

- Contribute heavily to technical forums and newsgroups
- Write blogs, articles, and even books
- Speak at user groups or conferences
- Lead local user groups, or put on free conferences
- Run community websites
- Beta test Microsoft software and provide feedback

When Microsoft recognizes a person as an MVP, they are recognizing the person's contributions to the community. Along with intangible benefits, such industry recognition, receipt of this award comes with many direct privileges and benefits, including:

- Access to a private MVP web site and news groups
- Access to private software betas
- The ability to contact Microsoft Product Managers and developers with specific questions
- Special training and conferences
- The ability to offer specific feedback on SQL Server

As of early 2009, there are about 270 SQL Server MVPs worldwide, of which about 80 are located in the United States.

How do you become a SQL Server MVP? It comes down to how much you contribute to the SQL Server community. Microsoft employees, and current MVPs, regularly monitor who is contributing to the SQL Server community,

Chapter 6: Participate in the SQL Server Community

and make MVP nominations based on these contributions. Periodically, teams within Microsoft review the nominations and make the selections. The MVP Award is made for a single year. To maintain the status of MVP, the MVP must continue to contribute to the community on a regular basis.

How Can I Contribute to the SQL Server Community?

Hopefully, by this stage, you are convinced of the many benefits of sharing your skills and knowledge with the rest of the SQL Server community. In this section, we'll look in more detail at each of the many different ways you can participate and contribute to the community. While not all of them may appeal to you, I am sure you will find one or more opportunities to help. These opportunities are not listed in any particular order. Just pick the ones that you find the most appealing.

Participate in Forums and News Groups

Participation in SQL Server forums (web-based) and news groups (NNTP-based) are the most common ways for a DBA to contribute to the SQL Server community. From here in, I will refer to both as forums, to reduce confusion. Answering (and asking) questions on these forums will provide many opportunities to learn from other DBAs.

There are many different SQL Server forums, each with their own personality. Some forums aren't very busy, while others are visited by thousands of people each day. Some forums are very business-like, while others are more relaxed. Some are well-moderated and encourage courtesy and respect at all times, while others are littered with flame wars. Most forums welcome newcomers, but a few (usually those dominated by a small "clique" of contributors), are not so welcoming. Some forums focus on specialty areas within SQL Server, while others are more general in their content.

I suggest you look around, find a forum you like and that suits your personality, and make it your home. By "home", I mean make the forum a place you visit regularly, both asking and answering questions. Personally, I feel it is better to have a home forum where you participate regularly, than to

Chapter 6: Participate in the SQL Server Community

participate in many different forums. The more you participate in any given forum, the more you become known and the better the rapport you will develop with other members of the forum community.

If you actively participate in a forum, you may eventually be asked to become a forum moderator. Or, if you want, you can volunteer to be a moderator. The duties of a forum moderator varies from forum to forum, but it generally involves taking a lead in answering questions, ensuring posts are categorized correctly, settling community disputes, and helping to keep spam out of the forum. However, the most important aspect of becoming a forum moderator is that you have been recognized as an outstanding contributor of the forum. Below are listed some of the most popular SQL Server forums:

Microsoft Public SQL Server Newsgroups

www.microsoft.com/technet/community/newsgroups/server/sql.mspx

Microsoft MSDN Public SQL Server Forums

http://social.msdn.microsoft.com/Forums/en-US/category/sqlserver

SQLServerCentral SQL Server Forums

www.sqlservercentral.com/forums/

SQL-Server-Performance.Com SQL Server Forums

www.sql-server-performance.com/community/forums/Default.aspx

SQLTeam SQL Server Forums

www.sqlteam.com/forums/

Participate in Social Networking Groups

Many social networking websites, such as Facebook, LinkedIn, and Twitter; have formal and informal SQL Server communities, where members ask questions, answer questions, or just socialize. If haven't become involved in either the SQL Server community, or social networking, then participating here can introduce you to both.

Chapter 6: Participate in the SQL Server Community

FaceBook

SQLServerCentral.Com Group:

www.facebook.com/home.php#/group.php?gid=32431988569

PASS Group:

www.facebook.com/home.php#/group.php?gid=20442293292

SQL Server Professionals Group:

www.facebook.com/group.php?gid=4465833121

LinkedIn

SQLServerCentral.Com Group: www.linkedin.com/groups?gid=72017

PASS Group: www.linkedin.com/groups?gid=61756

SQL Server Professionals Group: www.linkedin.com/groups?gid=54395

Twitter

SQLServerCentral.Com Group: http://www.twitter.com/SQLServerCentrl

PASS Group: www.twitter.com/sqlpass

Write and Share Scripts

One of the most valuable, but unsung, contributions you can make to the SQL Server community is to write and share useful Transact-SQL scripts. For example, if you have a clever script to kill all SPIDS, or a script to making backups easier, it's probable that other DBAs would like to see and use them. Many DBAs write their own scripts to make administrative tasks easier, and sharing them with the SQL Server community is a great contribution.

If you have scripts, how do you share them? There are many options. You can post them:

- In Transact-SQL script libraries available on some websites
- In forums
- On your own blogs, or other's blogs, or on your own website

Chapter 6: Participate in the SQL Server Community

If you want to make it easy for people to use your scripts, be sure to include a free public license as part of your code, as described at the Free Software Foundation website, at: www.fsf.org. This way, people know that it is safe to freely use your scripts.

However you share you scripts, they will be greatly appreciated by the SQL Server community.

SQLServerCentral.Com Script Archive

www.sqlservercentral.com/Scripts/

Microsoft Codeplex

www.codeplex.com

Join and Participate in a Local User's Group

Many cities have a local SQL Server user's group and/or a .NET user's group that you can join. User groups are a place where database and development professionals can get together and share their experiences, make new contacts, find out about new job opportunities, learn from presentations, socialize, and more.

Most, but not all, SQL Server user's groups are associated with PASS (Professional Association of SQL Server), an international organization for SQL Server professionals. Most local user's group members are either part-time or full-time DBAs, or SQL Server developers.

Some DBAs, especially DBA developers, choose to join a .NET users group instead. In fact, there are many more .NET user's groups than there are SQL Server user's groups. Most local .NET user's groups are associated with INETA, an international organization that focuses on .NET development.

There are many different ways in which you can participate with your local user's group. Some people attend for the learning and networking, and don't participate much beyond that. Others get more fully involved and help with leadership, marketing of the organization, managing the group's website, speaking at meetings, and even putting together day-long training events, such as SQLSaturday events, TechFests, or CodeCamps. Participation in user

Chapter 6: Participate in the SQL Server Community

groups is a great way to improve your people, speaking, project management, and leadership skills.

If you don't live in a city with a SQL Server or .NET user's group, consider starting your own. If you do decide to go this route, it's worth approaching either SQLPASS or INETA to have them help you start the group.

List of SQLPass.org Local User Groups

www.sqlpass.org/PASSChapters.aspx

List of INETA .NET User Groups

http://www.ineta.org/UserGroups/FindUserGroups.aspx

Join and Participate in PASS or INETA at the National Level

Besides getting involved in a local user's group, you can join and participate in PASS or INETA at the national level. Each year, both groups offer national conferences, in addition to smaller, one-day events. As with joining a local user's group, you can participate as a member, you can offer your services as a volunteer to help out at one of the national events, or you can volunteer to make a presentation at an event.

Some DBAs like to participate at both the local and national levels, while others prefer to participate in one or the other. If there is no local user's group you can attend, and you don't want to start up your own, then you may want to consider joining at a national level.

SQLPass.org SQL Server Users Group

www.sqlpass.org

INETA.org .NET Users Group

www.ineta.org

Chapter 6: Participate in the SQL Server Community

Speak at SQL Server Community Events

For the DBA who wants to speak and share his or her knowledge, there many of opportunities for you. For example, most user groups meet monthly, and as part of the meeting there will generally be a technical presentation. Given that there are hundreds of user groups, and most meet monthly, there are thousands of opportunities to speak. Besides user group meeting, there are special user group sponsored events, all of which need speakers. Some of these include SQLCamps, CodeCamps, SQL Saturdays, TechFests, PASS-sponsored events, INETA-sponsored events, and many more.

If you have little experience of public speaking, my advice is to start out small, and volunteer to speak at a local user's group meeting. This is a great way to get experience and establish yourself as a speaker. From there, you can move on to larger, regional and national events and conferences.

Bear in mind that most conferences have a restricted time period, often called a "call for speakers", during which interested parties can send in speaking proposals/abstracts for consideration. If you want to speak at these conferences, you will have to send in your proposals/abstracts using a specified format (which you can usually find at the conference's website), and during the specified timeframe. Some conferences pay a speaker a stipend and/or traveling costs, while others don't pay anything or cover any expenses (except, perhaps, free entrance to the conference).

Also bear in mind that the more popular the conference, the more competition there will be for speaking slots. Don't be discouraged if you don't get to speak at events such as TechEd or the PASS Summit the first time you submit speaking abstracts to them. To help maximize your chances of being selected as a speaker at a regional or national conference, first get some local speaking experience, select topics that are unique, and submit ideas across a range of different topics.

Speaking is a great way to not only participate in the SQL Server community; it is possibly the most effective way to establish a national reputation in your area of expertise (assuming this is one of your goals).

Chapter 6: Participate in the SQL Server Community

Below are some websites for events that require speakers:

PASS Community Summit

www.sqlpass.org

SQL Server Connections

www.devconnections.com

SQLTeach Conference

www.sqlteach.com

SQLSaturday

www.sqlsaturday.com

TechFests

www.techfests.com

DevLink Technical Conference

www.devlink.net

SQLBits (UK-based)

www.sqlbits.com

Write a Blog

Writing your own blog is a quick and easy way to begin sharing your knowledge with the SQL Server community. At little or no cost, and minimal setup, you can start blogging almost immediately. Blogs are a great way to share information, with their main strength and benefit being that they are highly interactive. Most blogs allow authenticated readers to comment on any blog entry, encouraging an often-lively two-way conversation between you and readers.

Some bloggers start up their own blog website using a domain name they select. If you want to really customize your blog and "make it your own", this may be a good option for you. The downside is that you have to market your blog so others find out about it.

Another option is blog at an established SQL Server-related blogging website. Most SQL Server community sites offer their members free blogs. While you

Chapter 6: Participate in the SQL Server Community

may not be able to customize the blog as you could with a blog you run yourself, it makes marketing it much easier, as you have a ready-made audience from the site where your blog is hosted.

Most DBAs who blog write about what they know best, namely SQL Server. They may write about new things they have learned, tricks of the trade, industry news, or their opinions on how a particular feature of SQL Server works. Blog entries can be short or long, technical or witty. Virtually any topic can be covered, using whatever writing style you prefer.

While blogs are a good way to contribute to the SQL Server community, a successful blog requires that you regularly contribute new and fresh content. If you only write one post a month, then it's likely that your blog will be visited rarely, and the conversation with your readers will die, which defeats the whole purpose of the blog.

So, if you decide to create your own blog, you must make a commitment to blog regularly – at least once a week. If you can't make that commitment, then consider some other way that works better for you, such as writing articles, where you can write and submit them at your leisure.

SQLServerCentral.Com Blogs

www.sqlservercentral.com/blogs

Simple-Talk.Com Blogs

www.simple-talk.com/community/blogs

Blogger.Com Free Blog Hosting

www.blogger.com

WordPress.Com Free Blog Hosting

www.wordpress.com

LiveJournal.Com Free Blog Hosting

www.livejournal.com

Write Articles

Writing articles on how to get the best out of SQL Server is a great way to share your knowledge with the SQL Server community. Unlike blogs, you

Chapter 6: Participate in the SQL Server Community

generally don't have to commit to writing an article once a week, giving you the opportunity to write when you have the time. Many novice writers start by contributing articles to smaller community websites, where the quality of the writing is not as critical, and where you seldom, if ever, get paid for your efforts. However, the main reason you are writing should be because you want to share your knowledge and to gain writing experience, not to make money.

If you are a good writer, then you can begin writing for larger websites, or even magazines, which pay for the articles you write. Pay for most articles tends to be in the $25.00 to $500.00 range, depending on the size and success of the website/publication, the length of the article, the originality of the article, and the writing quality of the article.

If you are interested in article writing, you should first check out the writer's guidelines of your chosen website or magazine. The guidelines will tell you what kind of articles they are looking for, along with how much they pay, if anything. Generally speaking, it is better to contact a website/publication with your article idea, to see if they are interested, rather than sending in articles on speculation.

If you don't have much writing experience, you may find that writing your first couple of articles is hard. However, the more you write, the easier it gets. In addition, many of the better quality websites and magazines will edit your work, sometimes sending the article back to you for a rewrite. Don't let this discourage you. Instead, use it as feedback you can use to improve your writing skills. If you need some writing tips, do an Internet search on "how to write articles" for lots of help.

SQLServerCentral.Com Writer's Guidelines

www.sqlservercentral.com/About/WriteForUs

Simple-Talk.Com Writer's Guidelines

www.simple-talk.com/become-an-author.aspx

SQL-Server-Performance.Com Writer's Guidelines

www.sql-server-performance.com/about/contribute.aspx

SQLTeam.Com Writer's Guidelines

Chapter 6: Participate in the SQL Server Community

www.sqlteam.com/writeforus.aspx

Write or Co-Write a Book

Writing a book is a huge undertaking. Back in the days of SQL Server 7.0 (or even 2000) it was not uncommon to see single-author books covering every aspect of SQL Server. The feature growth of SQL Server 2005 and SQL Server 2008, coupled with the relatively short shelf life of most SQL Server books (due to new software versions), means that most publishers now find a team of writers that can write the book as quickly as possible. Each author contributes chapters in their particular area of expertise.

This is good news for you, especially if you are not an established book writer, as this provides you with a greater opportunity to get involved in book writing. First, however, you need to become an expert in your chosen SQL Server specialty and, ideally, to have established yourself as a good writer. One of the best ways to do this is to get some published articles under your belt. With this combination of writing skills and technical knowledge, you can approach a book publisher and let them know of your strengths, and that you would like to participate in an upcoming book project.

Another way to get your foot in the book publishing door is to get to know existing SQL Server book authors, and ask them for guidance. Some of them may be currently working on a book project and know of co-writing opportunities that are available.

If you are really ambitious, and confident in your writing and technical skills, you can write a book proposal and send it to publishers for their review. You can propose to write the entire book (assuming you can do it quickly), or propose to write part of it, and even suggest people you know that might be good candidates as co-writers for the book.

Virtually all book publishers have writer's guidelines available. Before you contact any publisher, it is a good idea to read those guidelines so that you understand what the publishers are looking for. Each publisher is different and has different needs and interests, and you don't want to waste your time, and their time, on sending book proposals that don't interest them.

Chapter 6: Participate in the SQL Server Community

Red Gate Books

www.sqlservercentral.com/books/

Microsoft Press Author's Guidelines

www.microsoft.com/learning/books/author/default.mspx

Wrox Press Author's Guidelines

www.wrox.com/WileyCDA/Section/id-105073.html

O'Reilly Publishing Author's Guidelines

http://oreilly.com/oreilly/author/intro.csp

Start a Website

Of all the different ways you can participate and share with the SQL Server community, starting a SQL Server-related community website is one of the most rewarding, but also the most time-consuming. In fact, if you do it well, you may end up spending all your time devoted to managing and maintaining the website, which is pretty much what happened to me with the SQL-Server-Performance.com site I started, then later sold.

If you do an Internet search for SQL Server websites, you will find dozens of them. However, if you take a close look at them, you will notice that many have little content and aren't current. This is because lots of people dream of starting their own website, but once they do, and discover how much work it is, they stop, and the website dies.

- If you want to start your own SQL Server website, I have the following suggestions:
- Focus the website on a specific SQL Server-related topic that is not already covered by another website.
- Design the website so that it is easy for the SQL Server community to participate and contribute content.
- Learn everything you can about starting, managing, and marketing your website. There is plenty of helpful advice on the Internet.
- Ensure that you have 10+ hours a week you can devote to the website, week after week, month after month, year after year.

- Start small and don't invest a lot of money in the website until you know that you have an audience for your content, and the commitment to make the site work.
- Focus your energies on adding original content on a regular basis, rather than perfecting the design, look-and-feel, etc.

Mentor a Novice DBA

One of the best ways to develop your own knowledge, while helping others, is to mentor new and upcoming DBAs. These may be people at the organization where you are working, or it might even include DBAs you meet from your local user's group, or even a DBA on the other side of the world that you know through a SQL Server forum.

Mentoring need not take a lot of your time, but it may involve meetings, phone calls, and e-mails where you share information and offer career advice. There are many novice DBAs, and many of them would be delighted if you could help them out.

Summary: Participate in the SQL Server Community Today

Throughout this chapter, we have discussed the many different ways in which you can share your knowledge and contribute to the SQL Server community. In addition, we have seen the many benefits that come from doing so. If you are not already sharing your knowledge, start today. To get started, find a SQL Server forum you like and begin participating. Later, when you have time, find other ways to contribute. You will find that the time you spend helping others is time well spent. Ask any Exceptional DBA, they will tell you the same thing.

CHAPTER 7: MANAGE YOUR CAREER, DON'T LET IT MANAGE YOU

It has been my experience that many people tend to "fall into" their career, instead of making a conscious decision as to what their career should be. I know that this is what happened to me. I went to university to get a degree in journalism, but ended up with two degrees, one in Economics and another in Business Administration. When I began looking for a job, after graduating, the first job I was offered was selling computers in a retail store. Twenty-eight years later, my career is that of a Database Administrator. When I started university, or even after graduating, I had no idea where my career was going, or where it would end up.

I got to where I wanted to be in the end but, on reflection, I would have saved a lot of time, and a lot of money, if I had actively planned my career, even just a little bit. Sure, there is no way to anticipate every little twist and turn that the future will bring, but I think a little forethought and planning can help smooth out the inevitable bumps that all people face on their career path.

In this chapter, I am going to talk about how important it is to consciously manage your career, rather than let your career just happen to you. This is especially important if you want to be an Exceptional DBA. Maybe by following some of these tips, your career will be a little smoother sailing than mine.

Define a Career Path

The career of DBA offers many options. Instead of just coasting along, without giving much thought to what you want to make of your career, you need to become proactive and choose a long-term career path that meets your wants and needs.

Chapter 7: Manage Your Career, Don't Let It Manage You

The key to defining your career path is to be proactive. Decide what is important to you, and choose jobs that meet your needs. One way to be proactive is to ask yourself the following questions. Keep in mind that there is no right or wrong answer to any of these questions. Your answers will depend on your priorities and interests. However, by answering these questions honestly, you should have greater clarity on how you want to pursue your career as a DBA (or even if you really want a career as a DBA).

Do you want to be a Competent or an Exceptional DBA?

While the focus of this book is on how to become an Exceptional DBA, I understand that not everyone wants to make the required to become an Exceptional DBA. Many DBAs will be content on just being competent. There is nothing wrong with this, assuming it is a conscious choice. My challenge to you is to decide whether or not you want to be an Exceptional DBA, and then plan your career accordingly. In other words, make a conscious decision to be a competent or Exceptional DBA. Should you decide that you want to be an Exceptional DBA, I further challenge you to take immediate steps to start designing that career.

What DBA specialty do you want to focus on?

Have you picked a specialty to master? If you have picked a specialty, are you happy with it? Do you want to change it? You might try one specialty, and then decide it is not right for you. That's OK. The key is to be aware of your options, and find the specialty where you feel most comfortable.

Do you want to travel, or stay put?

Some DBA jobs require no travel, others a little travel, and others a lot of travel. Have you thought about how much travel you want to do? Your answer to this question can significantly influence which jobs you apply for and eventually accept. While many DBAs are family-oriented and like to stay home, there are other DBAs who jump at any chance to travel. In my current position as Director of DBA Education for Red Gate Software, I travel over 100,000 miles a year, visiting many cities and countries.

Chapter 7: Manage Your Career, Don't Let It Manage You

What size of a company do you want to work for?

Companies of all sizes need DBAs, although you will find the most opportunities at larger organizations. Do you have a preference as to the size of the company you work for? Many small companies offer growth opportunities as the company grows, but they often lack resources because all of their money is spent on growing the company. A large company is likely to offer many resources, but it might be bureaucratic and lack growth opportunities. Of course, every company is different, and you need to think about how you will fit into any organization where you're tempted to seek employment.

What kind of organization do you want to work for?

Do you want to work in a non-profit organization, an Internet startup, or an established multi-national organization? Different organizations have different working environments. Have you given any thought as to the industry you want work in? Would you be happier working for a government agency, an agricultural company, or a high-tech organization? I have talked to many DBAs working for government agencies who love their jobs because they like the stability of government work. If job stability is important to you, then a government job may be a better choice than an Internet startup.

What level of (seniority) do you want to attain?

In larger organizations, there may be many opportunities to advance. You might even have an opportunity to become a manager and lead a DBA team. Do you prefer to work for others and stay "hands on," or do you crave the challenge of managing others? If you do decide to become a manager, I want to challenge you to be an exceptional one. Why? Because there is a great shortage of exceptional managers in the industry. I have only met a small handful in my career, and an Exceptional DBA could easily become an Exceptional Manager.

Chapter 7: Manage Your Career, Don't Let It Manage You

Where do you want to work?

DBA jobs are located virtually everywhere, from small towns to large cities, from the inner city to the suburbs, and everywhere in between. Do you have a preference on where you want to spend your career? Do you want to work where you have access to the beach, the forests, or the mountains? Do you prefer hot or cold weather? Do you want to live close to family members, or do you want to escape them?

How much do you want to be paid?

You may think that you have little control over how much you are paid. It's true that you don't have full control, but you have more control than you think. There are many factors that determine how much you are paid. For example, the Exceptional DBA will earn more than the average DBA. Working in a large company or in a large city is usually rewarded with more pay. Likewise, a job that involves regular travel will often attract a higher salary. The SQL Server specialty you choose may also affect your earning power. Keep in mind that if salary is of great concern to you, then you will want to make choices that contribute to achieving this goal. Currently, DBAs who specialize in Business Intelligence can write their own ticket in many cases.

When do you want to retire?

Some people want to retire early, while others don't want to ever retire. Each person is different and views retirement differently. The DBA job you take can significantly affect when you might be able to retire. For example, an organization's pay scale, benefits package, and the cost of living in the area where you live all affect when you can retire. So if early retirement is an important thing for you, then plan a career path that will help you attain it.

Do you want to be your own boss?

Many DBAs prefer to work for themselves as independent consultants because they like being in complete control of their career. Other DBAs prefer the security that working for a company often brings. One option is no better than the other; they are just different. Decide what's most important to you, and then pursue the necessary steps to get there. One thing I have noticed when talking to many DBAs who have been consultants is that it is a career choice that can really wear on you. In other words, consultants have a higher than average burnout rate. Many consultants decide that it is not worth the trouble and return to being employees.

Do you have ambitions to become a SQL Server industry expert?

Many DBAs, even Exceptional DBAs, are content to limit their career, and the recognition they receive for it, to their place of work. Conversely, other DBAs like to see their career expand beyond their day-to-day work, using much of their free time to write, speak, or even do part-time consulting. You will learn more about this in the chapter called, "Managing your Online Brand."

Create a Plan and Set Goals

I recommend that you define what your long-term career plans are, and put them down on paper. Once you have decided where your career is going to take you, your next step is to set specific goals that define how you are going to get there.

Goals are specific actions that you will take in order to achieve your desired career path. When you define goals, keep the following criteria in mind.

Goals should be Short-Term

You can't predict the future, so it is best if you can keep goals short-term (a year or less). The shorter the time period you need to accomplish your goals, the lower the possibility of unexpected surprises getting in the way of you achieving them. For example, if you establish a goal that will take five years to accomplish, the odds of something happening within that five years to prevent you from attaining it are very high. By keeping goals short, they are more easily attainable. It is much better for your self-confidence to attain many short-term goals than it is to have fewer, longer-term goals that you may or may not reach.

Goals should be Specific

The more specific a goal is, the easier it is to attain. For example, a goal of "learning how to use Profiler to identify and troubleshoot SQL Server performance problems" is easier to attain than the goal of "learning how to use Profiler". If your goals are well-defined, and unambiguous, they will be more readily achievable.

Goals should be Realistic and Attainable

Any goal you set must be achievable within your given specification and time frame. For example, if you set yourself the goal of "learning how to use Profiler to identify and troubleshoot SQL Server performance problems" to a single weekend, then the odds of you meeting that goal are marginal. On the other hand, if you allow four weekends to accomplish this goal, then it is much more attainable.

Goals can be Small or Large

Just because a goal is realistic and attainable, it doesn't mean that it has to be small. If your goal is to change jobs within the next year, then this is a large goal, but one that can be achieved with the necessary planning and work.

Examples of Goals

To help you better understand what goals are, here are some examples of goals that are short-term, specific, realistic, and attainable:

- You want to learn how to master the Database Engine Tuning Advisor to tune indexes in the next 30 days.
- You want to improve your writing skills by writing a 2,000-word article on "SQL Server Backup and Restore Best Practices" to be published on a website within 90 days.
- You want to improve your speaking skills by making a presentation at the local user's group meeting next October.
- You want to update your SQL Server skills by attending a 1-week seminar next August on "How to Upgrade to SQL Server 2008."

Establish New Goals on a Yearly Basis

If you have a long-term career plan, then you need to break that plan down into a series of shorter-term goals, each goal forming an attainable milestone on your career path. An effective strategy is to establish a set of specific career goals on a yearly basis. By breaking down long-term plans into easily definable and attainable goals, attaining your overall career plan won't seem so difficult.

Take Action to Attain Your Goals

Many of us set goals, whether they are formal, written goals, as I have just described; or informal, unwritten goals, such as to read a certain book, to hike a trail, or to lose weight. As most of you know from personal experience, it is easy to let goals slip. Maybe you just don't have time, something else came up, you just don't feel like it right now, or you just plain forgot.

At the risk of stating the obvious, it's clear that if you want to manage your career, and not let your career manage you, then it's not enough just to create goals. You must also act on them. Goals don't fulfill themselves. It is only through your efforts that they will be realized. While I don't have any miraculous tips on how to accomplish your goals, here are a few that you might find useful:

- **Write each goal down on paper** (or at least in a word processing document). As part of this exercise, include any resources that you will need to accomplish the goal, the time schedule you want to achieve it in, and a description of why you want to accomplish the goal. The more thought you put into each goal, the more real it will become to you.
- **Post a list of your goals** somewhere close to you, so that you can see them every day.
- **Schedule your goals** as part of your appointment book. Don't just use Outlooks Calendar to schedule your regular job tasks, use it to schedule in time to accomplish your goals.
- **Enlist the help of others** to remind you about your goals, and to help you achieve them.
- **Use Web resources.** A simple Internet search on the key phrase "goal setting" will teach you a lot about how to set and attain goals.
- **As you complete a goal, check it off,** and then give yourself a little reward for accomplishing it, such as going out to eat, or seeing a movie.
- **Be persistent,** as may not attain your goal the first time around. If you don't, and the goal is still important to you, don't give up. Keep trying until you succeed.
- **Be patient.** Some goals take more work than others to attain. If you don't meet a goal, don't beat yourself up about it. Use it as a learning experience to do better at attaining the goal the next time you try.

Revaluate Goals and Long-Term Career Plans as Needed

A little earlier, I advised that you establish your goals on a yearly basis. Not only does this help you break long-term aims down into a set of short, attainable goals, it also helps you plan for change.

As time passes, your long-term career plans may change. This is normal, and expected. For example, you may get married, divorced, have a child, become ill, win a lottery, or experience one of many other things that can change your life for the better or worse.

Because your needs and wants change over time, your career plans may also change. In order to maintain control of your career, it is important that you periodically review your needs and wants, and alter your long-term career plans accordingly. This in effect will also affect your shorter-term goals, which may also need to change.

Essentially, you need to accept the fact that things will change. You must be aware of this, and make changes to your long-term career plans as appropriate.

Summary: It Takes a Conscious Decision on Your Part

You need to look out for your career, because nobody else is going to do it for you. If you want to be an Exceptional DBA, then you have to make a conscious decision to do that, and then accept full responsibility for how your career turns out. This means that you need to determine what kind of career path you want to follow, create specific goals to achieve these plans, and then work hard to make the goals reality. Don't beat yourself up if things don't always work out exactly as you want. Things change, and you need to plan time to reflect on your career path occasionally, revaluate it and change course if necessary.

CHAPTER 8: MANAGE YOUR BRAND WITHIN YOUR ORGANIZATION

While you may not think of it this way, the impression you create on other people within your organization will significantly affect how well you will succeed as a DBA. In other words, how the people you work with view you as a person can make all the difference between being an average DBA and being an Exceptional DBA.

I've worked with DBAs of wide-ranging ability and attitude. I've worked with people who always show up to work on time, don't mind staying late if they have to, constantly work hard to keep up with the ever-changing world of technology, and always follow through with whatever they promise to do. Conversely, I've also worked with several DBAs who come to work late, create a big scene if they have to stay late, know more about DOS than anyone else in the company, and can't be depended upon to follow-through with tasks that are assigned to them.

Which of these two types of DBA would you prefer to work with? Which of these DBAs has the potential to be an Exceptional DBA? In this case, the answer is obvious. Most people, however, fall within these two extremes of behavior, standing out neither as an Exceptional DBA, nor as a DBA that you would cross the building to avoid. In this chapter, we will explore some of the habits and attitudes that will help you develop a good reputation wherever you work, and move you towards the Exceptional DBA end of the scale.

If you are cooperative, hard-working, reliable and likeable then, of course, many more people will prefer to work with you. In addition, and critically so, many more people will also be willing to help you achieve the things you want to achieve.

Chapter 8: Manage Your Brand Within Your Organization

Developing Your Brand

If you want to succeed as an Exceptional DBA, then you need the help of others; you can't do it on your own. One of the best ways to get this help is to create a positive, personal image (brand, if you will) within the company. People tend to be drawn to "positive" people and to want to help them. This is, in my opinion, one of the most important things you can learn if you want to be an Exceptional DBA.

In other words, if you want to be an Exceptional DBA, you need to manage your internal brand in such a way as to present yourself in the best possible light. This does not mean faking characteristics in order to manipulate people. It means working hard, being honest and realistic about what you can and can't achieve, and generally adopting habits and attitudes that will help you work well with other people.

So, how do you set about achieving this? The following advice is designed to get you focused on some of the things you can do differently in order to improve your personal brand within your organization.

Focus on Business Goals

How many times have you heard something like the following, from a co-worker?

*"Why did management cut our budget? We don't have **enough** resources now to do our job."*

I have heard similar comments from co-workers at virtually every job I have ever had. When a decision, such as a budget cut, affects you directly, it is natural to accuse upper management of not knowing what they are doing. Of course, if they had any clue about what was going on, they would increase your budget instead of reducing it, right?

In some cases, your assumption may be right. Upper management doesn't always make the right decisions. On the other hand, if all managers were dim-witted, then most businesses would fail. However, this is not the case. Many businesses adapt successfully to changing market conditions, even if it means that difficult and unpopular decisions need to be made along the way. Over the long term, these businesses continue to thrive, producing more profits, adding more jobs, and generally helping the economy.

So what's my point? My point is that, as a DBA, you might not be privy to all the reasons why your organization's leaders make the decisions they make. For example, maybe the reason they are cutting your budget is to prevent layoffs. Alternatively, it may allow dollars to be freed up that can be invested in a new market that may be more profitable than your current market. In other words, what you may perceive as a foolish decision may actually be a great decision.

What does this mean to you? As a DBA, your focus should be on understanding the business goals of your organization, and helping it meet them. It is too easy to focus only on what you think the organization should be doing, or on the goals that are most attractive from your own team's point of view.

If you are facing a budget cut, don't complain or whine to others. Instead, focus on how you can get the most out of the budget you do have. If you are not clear on an organization's business goals, or why they have changed, then ask for an explanation. If you can build a very strong case that not cutting the budget is better for the organization than cutting, then by all means make it. Just because you agree to focus your efforts on helping your organization achieve its overall business goals, it doesn't mean you are a "yes" person. Most reasonable managers, if presented with documented evidence, can be persuaded to change their mind.

Ideally, you want to ensure that management understands your critical role in the business processes, so that you are involved in these decisions, rather than just being told about them. An average DBA is one that can keep the servers running. An Exceptional DBA is an integral part of the business processes and decisions related to them.

There are exceptions to this advice of course. If you find you work for a company of foolish managers, then I would suggest you start looking for a new job now, as the odds of the organization surviving long term are not great.

Chapter 8: Manage Your Brand Within Your Organization

Be a Leader, Take the Initiative

Many organizations are leadership wastelands. Nobody wants to take the lead or make critical decisions. Nobody wants to stand out, be a little different, or move out of their comfort zone. People often avoid taking the initiative because they are scared of failure, or that it might involve too much work, or because they worry that their peers may think of them as some sort of company suck-up. For these reasons, and others, many people actively avoid doing anything other than what they are told to do.

I admit that I have painted a pretty terrible picture. How would any organization ever grow and succeed if everyone felt this way? Fortunately, the picture is not quite as bleak as I've suggested and, in fact, should be seen as an opportunity for the Exceptional DBA to excel, by taking the initiative, and being a leader.

You don't have to become a manager to be a leader. You can be a leader in many different ways. Consider the following examples of an Exceptional DBA in action:

- On starting a new job as a DBA, you discover that all the disaster recovery-planning documents are out of date. You immediately volunteer to get them in shape.
- No formal complaint has been made, but several users have been grumbling about the slow performance of one particular SQL Server-based application. You take the initiative to investigate further so that the problem can be identified and corrected, before it becomes a serious issue.
- Your company is thinking about purchasing some new management software that could save many hours of DBA time. You volunteer to evaluate the software and write up a recommendation.
- Your boss mentions a new project that is coming down the pipe, and asks for ideas on how to implement it. Rather than leave it to others, you make time to do some thinking and research, and at the next meeting you offer your advice and suggestions.

A key element of good leadership is not waiting until you are asked. If you identify an area where you can help your organization, or help others in your organization, then take the initiative and do it. All too often, people see opportunities to help out, but don't do so because they figure someone else will eventually fulfill the need, so why should they.

Exceptional DBAs take every opportunity to help their organization, and thereby clearly differentiate themselves from those who don't care.

Volunteer for Hard or Undesirable Tasks

Whenever I start a new job, I take some time to figure out what jobs or tasks are critical to the success of the organization, and I make sure I'm prepared for them. At the same time, however, I also identify those tasks that nobody else seems to want to do, and volunteer to do them myself.

I've found that volunteering for "undesired tasks" can provide many benefits. The most obvious is that your manager and co-workers get to see right away that you are a team player and that you don't mind getting your hands dirty, and working hard. If you perform your work well, then people quickly learn that you can be depended upon.

Volunteering for the less popular jobs is also a good way to learn the inner workings of an organization. The more you know about how an organization works, the more you can contribute to it, and the more beneficial you become to the organization.

A less obvious benefit is that if you master the undesirable tasks, along with the critical ones, then you may become the only one who can perform, or want to perform, those tasks. This can make you invaluable to your organization, and can pay off in the long run. For example, you will be unlikely to be the first to leave during a lay off, and it can mean bigger raises each year. Once you have mastered these undesirable tasks, you should of course fully document your procedures, so that this knowledge is available to others in your organization that may need it.

Be careful though: don't just volunteer for any "unpopular" job. Only volunteer for those jobs or tasks that will allow you to grow in your position. While you might volunteer to do work others don't want to do, don't use this as an excuse to become stagnant. Instead, use it as a launching pad to perform even more critical and important tasks.

Have a "Get It Done" Attitude

As a DBA, you will be faced with many problems that need to be resolved. Never avoid problems and hope they will go away; they won't. The Exceptional DBA regards problems as challenges that need to be resolved now, not later. Likewise, the Exceptional DBA will never complain about a task assigned to him or her, or try to get out of it. The Exceptional DBA simply gets the task done as quickly and as effectively as possible.

Don't Spread Blame

In many organizations, many projects don't get completed successfully, and on time. The causes of this can be many:

- Management have the wrong expectations of the project,
- Not enough resources were provided,
- The time line was unrealistic,
- The team was not properly trained,
- The project leader was incompetent.

Who knows for sure? In many cases, it is probably some combination of actions or inactions that contributed toward the failure. When situations like this arise, many people's first reaction is to start blaming others. Not only does blame not contribute to making the project a success, it can also seed long-lasting bad feeling among many different people in the organization.

The Exceptional DBA doesn't spread blame. In fact, if the Exceptional DBA is involved in a failed project, he or she will acknowledge their responsibility for their part of the project and suggest ways to make the project eventually succeed, assuming it hasn't been cancelled. The Exceptional DBA realizes that spreading blame never helps, and does his or her best to make the project a success.

Accept Responsibility

There is no such thing as a perfect DBA. Everyone makes mistakes. The difference between average DBAs and Exceptional DBAs is that Exceptional DBAs accept that they are not always right.

When you make a mistake, don't try to cover it up, or blame others. Acknowledge it immediately and do whatever it takes to resolve it. For example, suppose that a new backup job you created failed overnight and so critical backups were not made. After discovering the mistake, the Exceptional DBA will accept responsibility, immediately determine what needs to be done, and do it. In this case, it might include making manual backups of the databases immediately and, later, when there is time, debugging the job so that it won't fail the next time it runs.

Don't Abuse your Power

In many organizations, the DBA is one of the most powerful and influential people in the IT department. This is a result of their responsibility of managing the organization's critical data, and ensuring that it is properly protected. As with any job that comes with responsibility and power, it can be abused. For example:

- As a DBA, you will generally have access to sensitive data. Never be tempted to use the data for any inappropriate uses.
- One of the responsibilities of a DBA is to be the guardian of the organization's data. This means that DBAs have some discretion as to who they allow data access. While exercising access control is an important practice, it can be abused. For example, some DBAs have been known to allow their favorite developers to have access to data they shouldn't have access to. In other cases, the DBA may prevent developers from accessing data they need to access to perform their job, just because they can.
- In many cases, DBAs have a stack of work that they need to do for others. DBAs must recognize that if they don't perform their requested tasks in a timely fashion, then others may be negatively affected. It is often up to the DBA to determine what work has the higher priority (or get others to help determine it), and proceed in a way that maximizes everyone's productivity. In addition, the DBA needs to be fair to others and not do favors for friends if they hurt the productivity of others.

The Exceptional DBA is fully aware of their power, and wields it in a way that is best for the organization.

Help Others Be Successful

One of my maxims for success, both as a DBA and in life generally, is this: "If you want people to help you get what you want, then you have to help other people get what they want." I am not talking about bribing people, or even trading favors. The Exceptional DBA likes to share his or her knowledge and experience, and one of the best ways to do this is to help others. When help is offered, it is done willingly, with no implication that it is a "favor," and no expectation of a return.

For example, if an end user is having problems logging onto a SQL Server-based application, then consider visiting the user in person and offering your help. If a co-worker is having trouble keeping up with his or her workload, see if you can volunteer to help do part of it. If a new DBA is hired, offer to become that DBA's mentor, helping them develop their DBA skills.

If you follow the policy of helping others when they need it, you will often find out that you will get many unexpected rewards. You never know who your next manager is going to be, and it might be the person you helped last week.

Avoid Office Politics

Many people allow themselves to be drawn inexorably in to the mystery and intrigue of office politics. Unfortunately, this is also a great way to make enemies and cause unnecessary division within an organization.

The Exceptional DBA keeps his or her ears open but, other than that, does his or her best to avoid the game of office politics. Sharing misinformation, rumors, or even false facts, is a recipe for disaster.

Downplay the Geek Factor

Let's face it, many DBAs are geeks. Some take pride in their geekiness, constantly reminding others of their geek status. Other geeks don't know they are geeks, but unknowingly spread their geekiness wherever they go. And then there are the geeks who know they are geeks, but try to avoid demonstrating the worse examples of geekiness. In other words, they try to fit in with non-geeks.

Geekiness doesn't really affect how one performs the technical side of one's job, but it can have negative consequences for the "people side" of the job. Unfortunately, geeks have been stereotyped with mostly negative characteristics, such as not being people-persons, not being able to talk in a language non-geeks can understand, acting or dressing a little "non-standard," and for boasting about their technical knowledge.

This perception of geeks may or may not be well-founded, but it exists regardless. Whether we accept this fact or not, most people like people who are like themselves. If you are the only geek in an organization of non-geeks, it can be a rough ride.

So what does all this mean to the Exceptional DBA? In my opinion, if you are a geek (as I am), and you want to become an Exceptional DBA, then you need to try to downplay the geek side of your personality. Ideally, by mastering the sort of soft skills that all Exceptional DBAs need, such as good people skills, you should be able to get along well with everyone, geek and non-geek alike.

Use Correct E-Mail Etiquette

In our high-speed, high-tech world, we are becoming more and more reliant on e-mail to communicate with others. This may not necessarily be a bad thing, but there are special considerations to using e-mail communication that don't necessarily apply to verbal, or more-formal written communications. For example:

- It is almost impossible to stop an email after you hit Send, though most of us have probably wished we could, at one time or another. For example, you are a little upset with your manager, or a co-worker, and you dash off a less than polite e-mail. After clicking the Send button, you realize that perhaps you did not take the proper amount of time to consider what you wrote, and its implications. Unfortunately, getting the e-mail back may not be possible. One colleague I work with has set up a rule in Outlook that keeps each outgoing e-mail in his outbox for five minutes before it is actually sent, just in case he has a change of heart after pressing Send. If you have a tendency toward firing off hasty e-mails, perhaps you should consider adding such a rule to your mail client.
- Once an e-mail has been sent, you lose control of its content. It can be forwarded to anyone, and sent anywhere. You probably don't want your

Chapter 8: Manage Your Brand Within Your Organization

honest assessment of a junior DBA shared with others in your organization. If you don't want something you have written in an e-mail to be seen by anyone other than the person to whom it was addressed, then don't send an e-mail. Deliver the message in person, instead.

- Many organizations archive every piece of e-mail that is sent or delivered via their e-mail system, so your e-mail can be read by others at virtually anytime. Keep your work and personal e-mail separate. Even personal, web-based e-mail can be intercepted and read by your organization if they are interested enough, and many are. One DBA I know, who sends and receives personal e-mail at work, only does so via his own personal Smartphone. That is the only way to ensure that your personal e-mail is not watched by your organization. Of course, Exceptional DBAs will minimize the use of work time for personal activities.
- If you are not careful, when selecting the "Send To" address for an e-mail, you might end up sending the wrong e-mail to the wrong person. I know one DBA who was looking for a new job, and sent a cover letter and resume to his current boss by mistake.
- Many people get in the habit of using e-mail for non-business purposes, such as sending jokes or off-color photos to co-workers. This has gotten many people into unexpected trouble. You will be best off my deleting any such e-mails you receive.

The Exceptional DBA is aware of the advantages of disadvantages of using e-mail to communicate. An Internet search on "e-mail etiquette" will provide many suggestions for improving your e-mail communications.

Participate in Meetings

Whether we like it or not, DBAs get many invitations to meetings. In some cases, it will be as a participant, other times as a presenter, and other times as the meeting chairperson. Whichever role the Exceptional DBA takes on, it should be taken on seriously. As a participant, the Exceptional DBA listens carefully, asks questions, and provides thoughtful feedback. As a presenter, the Exceptional DBA doesn't wing the presentation, instead preparing for it and, if appropriate, practicing it before hand. As the meeting chairperson, the Exceptional DBA only calls meetings that are beneficial for all attendees, starts the meeting on time, ends the meeting on time, uses an agenda to guide the course of the meeting, and takes notes to document any important decisions made in the meeting.

Make Presentations

Many DBAs are called upon to make presentations. They may be for company meetings, for training sessions, user groups meetings, or even speaking at industry conferences. Before making a presentation, the Exceptional DBA determines who the audience is, determines what the audience would like to learn from the presentation, outlines and develops the presentation, and practices the presentation before giving it to the audience.

Take Advantage of Learning Opportunities

Many organizations offer a wealth of training opportunities to their employees, covering both technical and soft skills training. This training may be conducted on-site by company trainers, or by contract trainers; it may involve attending a training center, it might be Internet-based, or it might include attending a conference. The Exceptional DBA takes advantage of all the training opportunities that are available. There is no such thing as an over-trained DBA.

Use Technology to make you More Productive

One thing that I have noticed about many experienced DBAs is that they tend to write their own scripts or applications to help make their jobs easier. If you have time, and there is no budget for commercial tools, then this may well be your only option.

However, in my opinion, too many DBAs are overly-reliant on their own home-grown scripts and applications. These tools often turn out not to fully meet the required purpose, or are hard to use, or need constant updating, to fix bugs or to provide more features, and they often aren't easily transferred to other systems. In other words, when you leave your job, whoever replaces you most likely won't be able to use the tools you created, and will have to go without, or have to write their own, which is a huge productivity drain.

Chapter 8: Manage Your Brand Within Your Organization

In my experience, most DBAs can boost their productivity by making optimal use of not only the native SQL Server tools, but also by available freeware (www.codeplex.com) or commercial tools. In many cases, buying a third-party productivity tool works out to be a lot less expensive than trying to write your own, and generally the commercial tool will be fully-tested, with some careful thought having been given to its usability. In addition, if one DBA leaves, then the replacement DBA can much more easily learn the tool and be immediately productive with it.

The Exceptional DBA fully understands how to use native SQL Server tools, but also keeps his or her eye open for other options. If a third-party tool is introduced that could greatly enhance their productivity, then they are willing to give it a try. Most DBAs are well-paid, and it is often better to spend a few extra dollars on tools to reduce "drudgery" work, in order to free up time for the DBA to work on more important tasks.

Be Internationally/Culturally Sensitive

The DBA community is made up of many different people who come from many different countries and cultures. While there may be a few DBAs who "don't fully embrace diversity," most do. DBAs, no matter where you work, come from many different places, each bringing their unique knowledge and experience to the DBA profession.

It is important that the Exceptional DBA is aware of cultural differences and takes them into consideration. This often requires cultural sensitivity and "bending over backward" to fully understand someone with a different upbringing than your own. While cultural differences may occasionally be the causes for differences of opinions, they are more often a great way to learn more about each other and the world.

Chapter 8: Manage Your Brand Within Your Organization

Summary: You Can't Be All Things to All People

There is no such thing as a perfect person, so there is no such thing as a perfect DBA. No matter who you are, or what you are, there will always be someone who doesn't like you. This is a fact of life. All we can do is to do the best we can with what we have been given.

Although we are not perfect, we can still go a long way to getting along well with others by managing our own brand. If you haven't already done so, take some time to figure out how your co-workers perceive you. You may discover that you get along well with everyone, or you may discover that you display some characteristics that some people perceive as less than ideal.

If you are not perceived the way you would like, then consider trying one or more of the suggestion in this chapter to help change how other's perceive you. It might take time, but if you are seeking to be an Exceptional DBA, then making the effort to manage your own brand, and taking the necessary time to allow changes to take effect, can be very rewarding.

CHAPTER 9: MANAGE YOUR ONLINE BRAND

In the previous chapter, we looked at how you can "manage your brand" within your organization. The chapter emphasized the importance of understanding the perception that others have of you, and taking steps to change or improve that perception, if necessary. You won't achieve this by manipulation, or adopting a false persona: you actually have to make the effort to adopt the attitudes and habits that mark out the dedicated, reliable and friendly DBA. If you do this, then you will find that you can more easily get along with others and, at the same time, people will be willing to help you accomplish your goals.

I mentioned in Chapter 7 that many DBAs are recognized, and well-respected, within their organization, but are not really known outside of it, and are quite content with that situation. However, if you have ambitions for broader recognition, or are looking for a new job or promotion, then it is becoming increasingly important that your "online brand" matches your internal brand. In other words, if someone were to do an extensive Internet search on you, would you like what they find? In this chapter, we take a look at how to manage your online brand.

What does it mean to "Manage" your Online Brand?

It is becoming increasingly common for people to conduct an Internet search to find out more about a person they propose to hire, or to deal with in some other business or personal capacity. This applies whether you are seeking a new job, a new consulting contract, selling something on eBay, or even dating someone for the first time.

According to a recent news report, people who wish to work for the city of Bozeman, Montana are required to include in their job application a list of all the websites to which they belong or have contributed, including social networking websites, forums, and more. Originally, they asked potential

Chapter 9: Manage Your Online Brand

employees for their usernames and passwords as well, but this request was later revoked, due to all the controversy it caused. While this is just one, admittedly extreme, example of an organization formally checking up on your on-line presence before hiring you, the fact is that the practice is becoming more and more common. As a rule, you should assume that any organization will check you out on the Internet before they hire you.

In the context of your professional career, you need to consider carefully what people will think of you after they conduct their search. Will you come across as a professional, or some kind of kook? Will they find a professionally written resume, or a MySpace.com webpage with a photo of you drinking with a bunch of your buddies at a bar, or an embarrassing YouTube.com video of you singing karaoke?

Whether you like it or not, most everything that goes on the Internet is available to virtually anyone who cares to look for it. This includes current web pages, as well as web pages that you thought had been deleted years ago, but were actually archived by a website such as the Wayback Machine (www.archive.org/web/web.php), which stores snapshots of websites, even those that no longer exist.

If you seek to become an Exceptional DBA, it is important that your online brand correspond with the image you want to get across to others. If you want others to consider you a professional DBA, then an Internet search should portray you that way. If it doesn't, you may have a hard time convincing people otherwise.

Here's an example. An employer is considering you and another person for a DBA position. The employer conducts an Internet search and finds this kind of information:

- **You**: Writes a SQL Server blog that is updated at least once a week; responds to dozens of forum questions in a professional way; has a well-designed and current resume; has a completed profile on LinkedIn.com; has pictures published on Flickr.com showing your most recent vacation.
- **Other Candidate**: Has published numerous, well-received articles on SQL Server websites; speaks at SQL Server conferences, responds to hundreds of forum posts, but has quite a demeaning attitude toward those asking questions; has an out-of-date resume; has a Facebook.com

Chapter 9: Manage Your Online Brand

page filled with lewd pictures and posts; and has a police report of being arrested for a DUI, as reported by a local newspaper.

Which of the two candidates do you think has the better chance of getting the job? Even if the other candidate is the more highly trained and experienced, I am going to guess that you have the better chance.

This might not seem fair from the other candidate's perspective, but what does fair have to do with it? As we have discussed before in this book, perception is a powerful influence, and if you don't project a positive image on the Internet, then it will be very difficult for you to convince people of your "Exceptional DBA" credentials.

Step 1: Discovering your Online Brand

To find out what your online brand is today, conduct a search on your name using several of the top Internet search engines. Use more than one, as not all search engines search all websites. When searching for yourself, enter your first and last name, surrounded by double-quote marks. If you have a common name, you may want to enter some other qualifying search string, such as your middle initial or name, the city and state where you live, where you went to university, or even the name of the organizations you have worked for over the years. When I search for DBA friends I know, I usually include the string "dba" or "sql" as part of the search in order to weed out others with the same name. Even with these additional search criteria, you may still have to wade through extraneous search results to find web pages that are actually about you.

Don't stop your brand search at the first ten web pages you try, as you might miss something important. I suggest you check out at least the first 50 search results (assuming you have that many), looking for pages that might include information on you. As you find web pages about yourself, bookmark them so you can return to them later for a closer examination.

As you review the web pages that contain information about you, try to classify them into one of the following three groups.

- Web pages that are current, accurate, and portray you in a positive light.

- Web pages that may be old, contain inaccuracies, and portray you in a positive light.
- Web pages, current or otherwise, accurate or inaccurate, which portray you in a negative light.

Ideally, you want most references to you on the Internet to fall into the first category. Those in the second category probably aren't a problem, but it would be better if they were updated and made accurate. If you have any references in the third category, then you will need to carefully evaluate each one, and determine how they might affect you if someone else sees them. If you have difficulty categorizing web pages in this fashion, consider having a friend take a look at them, for a more "impartial" appraisal.

What if you have a popular name and another person with the same name has a bad Internet reputation? How can you ensure that an employer, or prospective client, does not confuse the two of you? This is a difficult situation to overcome, but here are some suggestions:

- **Use your full name**, including middle initial (or full middle name). For example, Brad M McGehee is better than B. McGehee.
- **Pick a single way to "sign" your content**, and use it consistently. When you are applying for a job, or seeking work as a contractor or consultant, use that same name in all your contacts.
- **Include your photograph** with the content you control, such as your LinkedIn or FaceBook page.
- **Maximize the volume of your online content** as far you can, so that you feature prominently in search engine results for your name.
- **Include on your resume links to your online professional profiles**. If you are applying for a job, hiring managers will then know exactly where to look to find you.

I know of one DBA who shares a name with a convicted sex offender. If you are so unfortunate, you might specifically mention this to a hiring manager so they are aware of this before they find out on their own.

Step 2: Managing your Online Brand

Now that you know what your online brand looks like, how do you go about improving it? If all the web page references fall into the first category (current, accurate, positive), then you are in good shape and don't have to worry about your online brand hurting your ability to become an Exceptional DBA. If this is the case, you can skip on to Step 3, which explains how you can increase you online presence and brand, by getting more exposure.

However, what do you do if you're not so lucky, and you find references that fall into the two latter categories? In many cases, you will be able to directly alter any content that references you. For example, if you have a resume on a job site, forum postings, a personal website, a blog, a LinkedIn, MySpace, FaceBook, Flickr, Twitter, or other social networking presence, then you control the content. In these cases, simply modify them so that they are current, accurate, and portray you positively.

Changing web references that are not in your control can be problematic. If you have friends that have referenced you in a less than desirable way, on a web page they control, you can ask them to change it. In other cases, you may be able to contact the webmaster of the website and ask them to make a change to, or remove the offending content.

What if you can't remove or alter web page content that does not portray you positively? In this case, I suggest you counter-balance this information by expanding the quality and quantity of the online content that portrays you in a positive manner.

Step 3: Expanding your Online Brand

In the following sections, I'll discuss ways in which you can use the Internet to boost your online profile and improve your brand.

Websites

If you want to really differentiate yourself, one sure-fire way to do that is to build your own website. I am not talking about a personal website where you share pictures of your family or publish your poetry; I am talking about starting a SQL Server-related website. As I discussed in Chapter 6, setting up a website can be very time consuming, but is one of the best ways to create a really strong online brand.

Blogs

If a website is too ambitious for you, then creating a blog is the next best way to build your brand awareness and image on the Internet. Blogs generally take less time to manage and produce than websites, although they may take more work than you think. If you decide to write a blog, pick a subject matter area where you are an expert, and share your knowledge. Don't use the blog to launch personal attacks on the things in the world you don't like. Keep it professional, and focused on your work as a SQL Server DBA.

Forum Presence

If you are not doing so already, pick a SQL Server forum and spend time answering questions there. In order to boost your image, you will want to ensure that your posts are accurate and professional, and that you decline from participating in any flame wars. I know of one DBA who is a fairly popular consultant and who spends a lot of time posting in forums, but his attitude is so negative, that he portrays himself as a real jerk. If you can't be nice in forums, you are better off not even participating in them.

Social Networking Presence

Social networking websites are all the rage now and it seems like virtually everyone belongs to one or more of them. Social networking websites can be divided into two different categories: personal and professional, and I generally advise that you keep the two separate.

Personal Social Networking

Some of the more popular personal social networking websites include MySpace.Com, Windows Live Spaces, FaceBook.com, Flickr.com, YouTube.com, and Twitter.com, but there are many more. The main purpose of such sites is to allow you to share information among your friends and family. They are really not designed for professional use, although some users do include both personal and professional information on them. If you choose to use a personal social networking website, it is imperative that you evaluate the security settings of your account. Some of the websites, like Twitter, are wide open and everything you publish is available for virtually anyone to see. Other websites, such as FaceBook.com, have security settings that, in theory, prevent non-authorized users from viewing your content. However, the settings are quite complex and if you get it wrong, you may end up sharing your private messages with the entire world. This can be far from ideal, as you can be sure that if anyone is looking for information on you, they will be checking out these websites.

Professional Social Networking

Professional social networking websites are fewer in number, and are designed to help you establish an online brand, and develop new networking contacts. The most popular examples are **LinkedIn.com** and **Plaxo.com**, although PASS is also starting to offer networking capabilities through their website, **SQLPass.com**. These websites provide a means for you to create a network of professional contacts that you can use for whatever purpose you find suitable. For example, you might want to share with others what you are currently doing, to find a job, to advertise a job, to look for prospective customers, to ask a question or advice, or look for business deals. Another feature of these professional networking websites is that they allow you to create a professional profile, a resume of sorts, so that others are able to see what your credentials are, along with your work history.

If you currently participate in any social networking websites, I suggest you review your content to ensure that it portrays you in a professional manner and, if not, delete the potentially offensive content. If you currently don't participate, I would encourage you to check out several of the business-related sites, such as LinkedIn.Com, and create your own professional profile and web page. The more you make your presence felt on the Internet, the easier it will be for people to find and connect with you.

Online Resumes

Many DBAs have their resumes listed in one or more of the many job websites, or posted on their blog page or website. If you are looking for a new

Chapter 9: Manage Your Online Brand

job, or a consulting contract, then I suggest you keep them up to date so you can be easily contacted. On the other hand, if you are happily employed with no plans to move anywhere else, I would suggest you remove any resumes from the Internet. You don't want your current employer finding your resume on the Internet, as they may assume you are looking for a new job, even if you are not. The one exception to this would be your profile (a resume of sorts) on the professional networking websites, discussed in the previous section. If you are not looking for a new job, a career profile won't give the impression to your current employer that you are looking for a new job (unless, of course, you say that you are as part of your profile).

DBAs and Social Networking Websites

Up to this point, the discussion of social networking websites has been rather generic, and I'd like to use this section to provide some specific examples of how a DBA can use some of the more-popular networking sites to his or her advantage. If you currently aren't using social networking websites, the ones that follow are the best places to start, as you will find a lot of DBAs already using them.

LinkedIn.Com

LinkedIn is probably the most widely used professional social networking website for DBAs, and it offers several key features. For example, it allows you to:

- Create a network of other DBAs
- Create an online profile (resume), including details of your career and educational history
- Give and receive personal recommendations
- Enter details of current activities and follow the activity of your contacts
- Join other DBAs on SQL Server-specific groups. For example, you can join the SQLServerCentral.com group, or the SQLPASS group, where members can share information relevant to the group's "special interest"

Chapter 9: Manage Your Online Brand

If you only sign up for a single social networking website, this is the one to use.

FaceBook.Com

While FaceBook is a personal social networking website, many DBAs use it to keep connected to other DBAs in the SQL Server community, most of whom they know personally. Many DBAs find it a great way to keep up-to-date with their personal contacts and enhance their on-line brand. I personally recommend keeping personal and professional social networking separate, but FaceBook it is one of those sites where it's easy to break this rule.

Twitter.Com

Twitter is a personal social networking website that has exploded in popularity with DBAs who have found it a valuable way to develop a "support network" of friends and fellow DBAs. The basic premise of the site is to let your "followers" know what you are doing right now, though its use is expanding beyond that, to the asking and answering of technical questions, and general conversation. As such, it tends to provide a hectic mix of personal and technical information.

Keep in mind that your "tweets" can be read by anyone, including your current employer, and any future employers, so I caution you to think about what you share on Twitter.

SQLServerCentral.Com

Although you may not automatically classify SQL Server-related websites, such as SQLServerCentral.com and others, as social networking websites, in many ways that is what they are. SQLServerCentral has very active forums where social networking occurs on a daily basis.

SQLPASS PASSPort

SQLPASS is the Professional Association for SQL Server Professionals. Membership of this international organization is free and open to all SQL

Server DBAs. Once you have joined, you can complete a PASSPort, which is a profile similar to that which you'll find on LinkedIn, but much less flexible and extensive.

If you are a member of PASS or are interested in volunteering for PASS activities, such as speaking at the annual PASS Community Summit, you should have a PASSPort profile. You won't even be considered as being a speaker at the PASS Community Summit unless you have a completed an up-to-date PASSPort.

Projecting a Professional Image on the Internet: Dos and Don'ts

Most DBAs probably feel they can decide for themselves what is and is not appropriate behavior on the Internet, so a list of "dos and don'ts" may seem a little unnecessary. However, as I hinted earlier, there are some grey areas, and some sites where it's very easy to get "carried away" and post information that you later regret.

So, if you feel like you'd benefit from a little advice on how to project the best-possible online image, I offer you my "Internet dos and don'ts". I'll admit that my advice errs on the side of cautious and conservative, but then so do many hiring managers.

Do...

- **Keep your professional life and personal life separate**. Create separate blogs for professional and personal posts; don't mix them together on one blog.
- **Be careful about what you post**. Only share personal content on websites that offer some degree of security, and only allow friends and family to access it. Even then, keep in mind that there is no such thing as "absolute" security and privacy so don't post any content that you wouldn't want a potential employer (or your mother) to see.
- **Use your full name** whenever you post professional content on forums, newsgroups, blogs, articles, and so on. You want people to be

able to easily find you, and the best way to do this is to use your full name as your "personal brand".
- **Post professionally-taken portraits** so that others can see what you look like.
- **Create profiles at professional social networking websites**, such as Plaxo.com, LinkedIn.com, SQLPass.org, or similar, and keep them up-to-date. This makes it easy for other DBAs, and perhaps hiring managers, to find you, and find out what you know, and what experience you have. You don't want to miss out on a potentially lucrative job opportunity due to old or incomplete information.
- **Maintain an up-to-date online resume, when job seeking.** You can post it on a job website, networking website, or professional blog.
- **Participate in professional forums, newsgroups and blogs**, where you have the opportunity share your knowledge and help others.
- **Be professional, culturally sensitive, considerate, and helpful**, in all forum and newsgroup postings.
- **Assume that everything you post will be seen by everyone**, and for a long time to come. Once you post content on the Internet, you lose control over it.

Don't…

- **Use a "cute, clever, or funny" alias** (or user name) to refer to yourself professionally. No matter how amusing, aliases such as "SQLSanta" or similar, don't tend to make a good impression on hiring managers or potential clients. If you do choose to use one, try to use it exclusively for personal social networking, and use your proper name for professional social networking. However, unless you really can maintain a clear distinction between the two (and it is difficult to do this), then I advise that you avoid cute aliases altogether.
- **Post "unprofessional" pictures or videos** of yourself or others. I have seen tasteless photos and videos of DBAs on the Internet. When these are first posted, they might seem a little amusing, but they won't be amusing to a hiring manager.
- **Share links to URLs that include potentially offensive content**. I have seen this problem on Twitter a lot. What may be amusing to you could be regarded as bad taste by others.

Chapter 9: Manage Your Online Brand

- **Embellish the truth in your professional profile**s, biographies, or when creating resumes. The truth will always catch up with you.
- **Engage in forum or newsgroup flame wars** – be courteous and helpful at all times, regardless of the "provocation".
- **Use "adult" language anytime, anywhere.** It is likely to offend.
- **Disparage or attack others.** If you disagree with someone's views, or simply don't like them, ignore them. In more than one case, I have seen forum posts or blog entries that attack a person by name. Not only is this unprofessional, it could be unlawful.
- **Write anything that you don't want your current employer to see.** For example, don't criticize or ridicule them, or share confidential information about your organization.

Summary: Start Managing your Online Brand Today

If you have not already done so, conduct an Internet search on yourself as soon as you find time. If you find any content that is less that flattering, and that you can change, then do so as soon as possible. If you can't change the content directly, then put in requests to get the changes made. If your online presence is weak or needs improving, take the initiative and begin building it today.

Chapter 10: Get An Exceptional DBA Job

As an Exceptional DBA, you may find yourself in the position of looking for a new job. This will generally happen for one of three, broad, reasons:

- **Forced unemployment** – your organization fails completely (or is on the brink), is downsized, or "restructured". In other words, you have been, or are about to be, laid off. One could also include here situations where the DBA feels compelled to move on due to "unreasonable" or "unethical" behavior on behalf of their employer.
- **Career advancement** – you feel you've hit the "ceiling" in your current employment, either in terms of pay, advancement possibilities or professional challenges. Sometimes, the nature of a given business means that there is limited scope for variety, or fresh challenges, and the DBA feels he or she is getting "stale". Other times, the organization may simply not appreciate the value an Exceptional DBA can bring to it.
- **Personal Choice** – there are numerous personal reasons why a DBA may decided to "move on", from a need to relocate, perhaps to follow a partner or spouse; to a simple desire for a new direction and set of challenges.

Whatever the reason for a DBA's need to find a new job, I hope that this chapter can offer useful advice on how to make the transition a little bit easier. I'll discuss how to sever ties with your previous employer in the most professional way possible, whether you're leaving by choice or otherwise; how to find and get the new job that your talents deserve and, finally; how to make the best impression when you arrive in your new job. In each case, I try to offer advice specific to the Exceptional DBA, rather than generic tips on writing effective resumes, or preparing for interviews.

Finding a new job will generally be quite stressful, but if you make the right choices then the financial rewards, or a more challenging and satisfying new job, will be more than adequate compensation.

Chapter 10: Get An Exceptional DBA Job

Leaving Your Old Job Behind

Whether you are laid off, or quit voluntarily, it is always a best practice to leave on a high note; you should strive to create the best-possible final impression. If you have enjoyed your old job, this will come naturally. If your departure is enforced, you need to override any potential feelings of unhappiness or resentment, and make an effort to leave on good terms.

Why? First, your former manager (and co-workers) may be contacted by prospective employers for references. Such references can make or break your chances of landing a new job. Some organizations have policies in place that restrict what can be said in references but, if you've failed to leave on good terms, then any references are likely to be far from glowing.

Second, you never know who you may be working with in the future. If you're departing in unhappy circumstances, it's tempting to adopt a "goodbye and good riddance" attitude, but this is a mistake. The DBA "world" is relatively small, and the odds that you will end up working again with people you have worked with in the past, is higher than average. This has happened to me twice during my DBA career. In both cases, fortunately, I had parted on good terms with these people, and one of these former co-workers ended up doing me a big favor that was very financially rewarding.

If the above two reasons aren't enough to encourage you to leave your old job on good terms, here's one more: personal pride. I don't know about you, but it makes me feel good inside whenever I do the right thing, and leaving a positive final impression is one of those "right things".

Voluntary Job Moves

When you are looking for a job while still currently employed, it is natural that some of your attention and energy will be diverted towards this new venture. However, it is important that you do everything possible to minimize the impact of this on your current job. You should strive to maintain your same high standards, and restrict your job seeking activities to your own time.

Chapter 10: Get An Exceptional DBA Job

> **NOTE:**
> Remember to tell prospective employers that you are currently working and you don't want them to contact your current employer. This is a common request of prospective employers that they normally abide by.

Once you've secured a new position, there are several points to consider with regard to your notice period, resignation process, and transition. If you get them all right, you will create a good, and lasting final impression on your old employer. Then, rather than leave "under a cloud", most likely you will be given a going-away party by your co-workers. In my last job, about 40 people (half of the IT department) attended my going-away party, including the Director of IT, who was two management layers above me. This was a great feeling, and this is the kind of happy ending you want when moving from one job to another.

Notice Period

Give your employer as much notice as you can. The exact length of notice period varies by organization, but the industry standard is to give at least two week's notice. Check your employment contract, or your organization's general policy with regard to notice periods, but I would recommend giving at least a four week notice period, and preferably more if circumstances, such as the start date at your new job, will allow it.

It will often take your employer a significant amount of time to find a suitable replacement. In an ideal world, you would turn in your resignation with a large lead time, your replacement would be hired, and you would still be around long enough to train him or her. This rarely happens, but if you can pull it off, your former organization will greatly appreciate it.

Resignation Process

Make the resignation process as personal as possible. Here is what I recommend. First, put together a resignation letter that states when you are leaving, why you are leaving, and how much you have appreciated working for the company. Include a transition plan to help make it easier for your organization to replace you, with suggestions on how to cover your duties during any interim period between you leaving and the new hire arriving.

Chapter 10: Get An Exceptional DBA Job

Don't send the resignation letter via e-mail, or as a paper memo; instead, schedule a meeting with your manager and give it to him or her in person, and talk about what is in the letter. Keep the conversation personal and upbeat, especially emphasizing how you intend to make the transition as easy as possible for the company. In most cases, your manager will greatly appreciate your consideration, professionalism and personal touch.

Transition Period

Once you have announced your resignation, start taking the necessary steps to ensure there is a smooth transition. This may include writing or updating documentation, and training others to perform your current job duties. Ideally, you will be training your replacement, but it may equally well be that you are training co-workers to cover your duties for an interim period until your old position has been filled. Either way, you should do everything you can to help make the transition as smooth as possible.

I have noticed, from personal experience, that once someone turns in their resignation, he or she often tends to consider their job to be "over" and they become a "short-timer". This is an unprofessional attitude, and could easily leave a negative impression with your manager and co-workers. You are being paid for every day you are at work, and you want to ensure that your old organization is still getting value for what they are paying you for.

Requesting Recommendations

Assuming that you have done a good job of making the resignation and transition process as smooth as possible, ask your manager for a formal recommendation letter, or perhaps a recommendation on a social networking site, such as LinkedIn.

While much of your effort will be spent working with your manager during the transition, don't forget your co-workers. You also want to part with them on a friendly basis and, if appropriate, you can certainly ask a few trusted co-workers for personal recommendations. In most cases, they will be glad to do so.

Chapter 10: Get An Exceptional DBA Job

What to do if you are Laid Off

Even an Exceptional DBA can be laid off. While you have control over your skills and the choices you make, you have little control over how your company is managed, or how it chooses to try to alleviate any financial difficulties.

Being laid off is not fun, and it can be a huge financial and psychological blow. However, the Exceptional DBA will still take all reasonable steps to make the forced separation work, to his or her advantage. It is possible you will be feeling ill-treated, but that is not the point. You need to consider how your actions, under this time of duress, will affect you at some future point. By being as professional as possible now, you will reap later rewards.

Most of the previous advice about transitioning and requesting recommendations applies here too. Assuming you are not escorted out the door shortly after being laid off (which is a tacky thing for any organization to do, unless of course you are being fired for gross misconduct), ask for a meeting with your manager, and discuss what you can do to make the transition as smooth as possible. If you handle the situation as professionally and amicably as possible, it may well have certain additional benefits:

- Your manger may assist you in getting you the best severance package available.
- You may be able to negotiate a longer period between being informed of your impending redundancy and your "final day". This will give you additional time to find new work.
- You will receive good recommendations from your manager and co-workers, which will be important in your new job hunt.

Sometimes, an organization will lay off staff to cut costs, and then quickly realize that critical tasks simply aren't getting done. It is not uncommon for them to try to fill the skills gap by re-hiring previous employees on a consulting basis. While you may not want to stay on as a consultant for very long, it does offer the benefit of financial stability, as you search for permanent work. However, by the same token, it could also divert your energies away from this search. In any event, if this option appeals to you, be sure to tell your manager of your interest.

Chapter 10: Get An Exceptional DBA Job

In most ways, if you are laid off, you will want to treat the situation similarly as if you are resigning of your own accord. The only real difference between the two is who makes the decision, you or your organization. Once you overcome the shock of it happening to you, it's time to get busy and find that next DBA job.

The Job Search

The best strategy, where possible, is to begin your job search before you quit your current job. If choice or circumstance dictates that you quit your current job first, and take a break before starting a new one, then my advice would be to keep the length of time between jobs as short as possible.

Job searches can take weeks, or even months, and you probably don't want to be unemployed for a lengthy period of time, as employers tend to favor job candidates whose skills and experience are up-to-date. If you are currently employed in a similar role, then it gives the prospective employer a greater degree of confidence that you can perform the necessary tasks. Furthermore, the ability to negotiate a new job offer while still currently employed is a position of relative strength; it means you are "in demand". Also, if you can't negotiate the employment package that best meets your needs, you still have a job to fall back on.

Finding a new job is really a two-step process:

- Identify potential job opportunities
- Carefully vet each opportunity to see if it meets your needs

In other words, you generally don't want to take just any old job that is available and offered to you. You only want to accept a job offer from an organization that can meet your professional and personal requirements, as an Exceptional DBA. Choosing the best option sometimes involves a "trade off" between factors such as working hours, pay, professional development opportunities, and so on. In order to make the right choice, you need to be very clear up front what you are looking for in your new job. For example, which of the following are most important to you?

- Salary
- Bonus opportunities

- Stock options
- Benefits
- Vacation time
- Work hours, both how many, and when. Is flexi-time an option?
- Option to telecommute
- The job's physical location
- Opportunities for advancement
- Interest level and variety of the work
- Corporate culture
- Learning opportunities (Does the organization pay for training and conferences?)
- The size, reputation and financial stability of the organization
- The people you will be working with
- The roles and prominence of existing DBAs within the company (in other words, an indication that the company understands and appreciates the contributions of the DBA)

I suggest you create your own list of the "ideal characteristics" for a new job. While you will never to be able to get everything you want, you still need to establish a list of criteria so you can better determine how close a particular job comes to your ideal. If you are fortunate enough to be considering multiple job opportunities, consider creating a spreadsheet so you can more easily compare one opportunity to another.

If you have been laid off for a while, and job offers are sparse, you may have to accept any job that is offered to you. If that's the case, first count yourself lucky to have a job at all, and then be patient. Work on your skill set, widen your personal and social networks and, as time passes, keep your eyes open for a job that is better suited to you.

Finding an Exceptional DBA Job

If you are like me, then you will find hunting for a new job to be about as much fun as having a cavity filled by a dentist. It's one of those undesirable tasks that everyone has to experience a few times in their life.

Fortunately, the Internet has, to some extent at least, eased the previously-painful process of looking for a job. I can still remember the "old days" of scouring classified job ads in the back of newspapers, and sending out unsolicited resumes, via snail mail, to the HR departments of prospective companies.

Today, there are many different ways to identify potential job opportunities, and I'd like to split the techniques down into two basic categories. The first category is what I term "conventional job hunting", which basically involves hearing about a job vacancy, assessing its suitability and then applying for it.

The second type of job hunting is proactive, and involves identifying organizations you would like to work for and starting to build a business relationship with them, regardless of whether or not they are currently hiring. The idea is that you will be "top of their list" when they do begin hiring, or you may even be able to convince them to hire you, even if they don't realize at the time that they need you! This is what I call "proactive job creation".

Conventional Job Hunting

Much has already been written about the process of "conventional" job hunting and about the relative merits or otherwise of the various job websites, technical recruiting firms, and so on. Job websites such as Monster.com, or Dice.com (which is more focused on technical jobs), do offer a lot of DBA jobs. However, there is also a great deal of competition for these jobs, as they are searched by a large number people. You also may want to check out Craigslist.com, and job listings on various SQL Server-related websites, such as SQLServerCentral.Com.

Your first port of call, however, should be the websites of companies that interest you. Often, jobs are offered on an organization's website before they advertised elsewhere. Placing job wanted ads is expensive for companies and, to cut costs, many companies rely more or less exclusively on their company website, to advertise available positions. Of course, this won't tell you about un-posted jobs, but more on that shortly.

Technical recruiting firms can often provide opportunities you may not be able to find elsewhere, but can be a pain to deal with, in my experience. Technical recruiters make a commission on the jobs they can fill, and so their primary goal is fill as many jobs as possible; not to find you your ideal job. As such, they sometimes waste your time by sending you on interviews for jobs for which you are not really suited. In addition, they are often seeking contract workers (temporary jobs), which may or may not be what you are looking for. If you decide to work with a recruiter, be sure you are very

Chapter 10: Get An Exceptional DBA Job

specific in telling them the type of job you are looking for. Lastly, don't sign a contract with a recruiter. Their contract is with the employer, not you.

While general job websites and recruiting firms can sometimes fill a need, the Exceptional DBA's greatest asset when seeking a new job is, undoubtedly, the strength of their professional and social networks. The Exceptional DBA, throughout their career, will make time to participate in the SQL Server community, to attend conferences and user group meetings, and to build a strong online brand, and professional network.

> **NOTE:**
> If you've not yet done these things already, make sure you read chapters 6, 8 and 9 of this book, and get started right away.

Even "conventional" job hunting does not just mean sitting around waiting for job opportunities to come to you. It is through social network groups, such as LinkedIn, or at user group meetings, that you will find out about many DBA positions, often before the job is "officially" announced. Even if specific jobs are not discussed, you can let others know you are looking for a new job, and there might be hiring managers or technical recruiters in the audience you can speak with.

I got my current job through my personal network of contacts, and I strongly recommend that use your own network to find out about available DBA jobs. You can also use these same contacts to find out more about these jobs, so you can better determine if they meet your needs and wants. Additionally, it is always a plus to have someone recommend you, rather than sending in a resume that will probably end up in a large pile of other resumes, on someone's desk.

With the help of your personal network, you can also take your job hunting a stage further and attempt what I refer to as "proactive job creation".

Proactive Job Creation

The approach I will describe here is slightly more "non-standard", and is applicable mostly to those Exceptional DBAs who are currently working and have plenty of time to conduct a job search. As noted earlier, passively waiting for the "right job" to appear is not necessarily going to get you the job

Chapter 10: Get An Exceptional DBA Job

that best meets your wants and desires. Instead of waiting for jobs to come to you, you must go out and seek the jobs yourself.

You must talk to your personal network of contacts, as described in the previous section. Tell them that you are looking for a new job, and that you would appreciate if they could let you know of any jobs that are currently open; or if there is nothing available now, for them to keep their ears open for openings in the future. It also means actively approaching companies you would like to work for, regardless of whether they are currently advertising any job opportunities. Having identified some companies that interest you, check out the company's website to see if any jobs are listed. If no jobs are listed, as will often be the case, there is still useful action to take. There may be job opportunities that have not yet been posted and, if there are, you want to be the first to find out about them.

A good first step in this process is to identify the organization's IT Director (or some manager in the IT department) and send a cover letter and resume (snail mail or e-mail), asking about possible DBA positions in the company. You can state in your letter that you are interested in making a move, and that you would like to know if there are any DBA jobs available, or to be kept in mind if any become available in the future. Your goal is to try and develop a business relationship with the hiring manager. Your letter should clearly state the reasons for your specific interest in their company, along with the skills and experience you can offer, and how you think that would benefit them. Who knows; you may even be able to convince the company of the need to hire you, even if they had no immediate plans to advertise for such a position.

A slight variation of this tactic is to contact a DBA, or other IT worker, who already works for a company you are interested in, and ask their advice for seeking out a DBA job at the organization. Many companies give their employees financial bonuses if they recommend a new employee, and many employees are willing to help you out, assuming you are cordial and professional. You can often identify specific people by calling the company and asking to speak to a DBA, or you can use the Internet to search for people who work for the same company. If you have difficulty identifying people in the IT department directly, get advice from your personal and social networking contacts, on whom to contact in regard to DBA jobs.

In many cases, a DBA job won't be immediately available, but your strategy should be to begin making the proper connections and developing a professional relationship with organizations that you admire and would like to

Chapter 10: Get An Exceptional DBA Job

work for. That way, when an Exceptional DBA job does become available, you will know about it, and you will have already laid the groundwork.

As you can see, this will not be a quick or easy process, especially if there are currently no existing positions available. But if you have the time, this approach can be highly effective in helping you identify DBA jobs at organizations that you admire.

Assessing an Exceptional DBA Job

When a job opportunity does arrive, the effort and research that you put into your job hunt will stand you in good stead. However, there is still more work to be done to ensure that the job and the company really do meet your needs and expectations. You will want to find out as much "inside" information as you can in order to be sure that this is a job offer you'd like to accept.

As a start, you will examine the company's website, and talk to any of your contacts, in social networking groups or user groups, who may have some experience of working in or with the company. However, at the very minimum, you will also want to:

- **Perform a general Internet search** of the company to see what turns up. Check out news websites, review websites, and any forums that might cover the organization.
- **Review the organization's annual report**, assuming you are applying to work for a public company. It will usually be available on their website and will tell you if the company is growing, stagnating, or failing. If reading annual reports fills you with dread, some of this information is often summarized on the various financial websites.
- **Get a tour of the organization**, and find out exactly where you would be working. If they show you a grey cube set among several hundred other grey cubes, then this job may not be for you. I know I wouldn't work for that sort of company.
- **Interview your potential new manager**. Often, this will be the person who interviews you and makes the hiring decision, but not always. If you have received a job offer from someone other than who will be your new manager, be sure you find out who your manager will be, and talk to him or her. Interviewing your prospective employer may seem a little forward for some people, but it is very important. How else will you be able to get answers to many of your questions? Besides, your

Chapter 10: Get An Exceptional DBA Job

questions will be a clear indication to the people you talk to at the organization that you are taking your job search seriously, and are not desperately seeking any employer who will take you.
- **Talk to your potential co-workers.** If the company is large, try to meet the IT director and other people you will be working with. If the company is small, try to meet the owner or the general manager of the location where you will be working.

It may seem like a lot of work to check an organization out before you accept a job offer, but it is the only way to be sure that the job is the right one for you. The more time you take to properly researching your job opportunities, up front, the happier you will be in the long run with the job choices you eventually make.

Applying for the Job

While I have covered a lot of job hunting advice already, I also want to include two additional sections where I'll offer specific advice on how the Exceptional DBA can best present his or her skills on their resume, and then survive even the most-grueling of interviews.

Chapter 10: Get An Exceptional DBA Job

Tips for Writing a Resume

During most job searches, you will be asked to submit your resume (or a C.V. if you don't live in the United States). In some cases this may be a mere formality, as in the case where the hiring manager personally knows you, or when you have been highly recommended by someone the manager trusts. In these cases, your resume won't count for much, assuming anyone bothers to read it. It is the strength of your contacts that has gotten you this far. In other cases, you won't have any contacts in the organization and your resume may be the only opportunity you have to impress a hiring manager.

Depending on the desirability of the job, location, the current job market conditions and how aggressively the job opening has been marketed, there may be only a few job applicants, or there may be hundreds. In the former case, it's likely that your resume will get careful consideration. In the latter, it will *only* get careful consideration if it stand outs from the crowd and shouts "I am an Exceptional DBA", without you ever having to actually say it.

> **NOTE:**
> There are literally hundreds of book and website articles on how to create a great resume, so I'll try not to repeat what has already been written, although this is not entirely avoidable. Do a web search on the phrase "how to write a technical resume" to out more about this subject.

The Basics

Most of the advice in this section should "go without saying", but it is surprising how many people get even the most basic things wrong. When you submit a resume, find out the format the organization wants it in. They may prefer paper, an e-mail, a Word file, a PDF file, HTML, or they may have a special online resume form. If you don't provide your resume in the correct format, it most likely will be ignored.

Regardless of the required format, a resume should include the following information, at a minimum:

- **Contact information**. If you can't be contacted, it's safe to say you won't get the job.

- **The specific position you are applying for**. You would also include this in a cover letter, but it's best to have it in both places in case the cover letter gets lost.
- **Education**. Keep in brief, especially if your education is not technology related.
- **Technical certifications**. Only if they are relevant to the job.
- **Technical awards**, such as Microsoft's SQL Server MVP award, or the SQLServerCentral.Com "Exceptional DBA" Award.
- **Work experience**. This is the most important part of your resume and is covered in detail in the next section
- **Community Work**. If you have room on the resume (and perhaps if you don't yet have a lot of practical experience), you may also want to include details of your involvement with SQL Server community sites, user groups and so on. This information is optional, and the space used for this is probably better spent describing your work experience.

There are several other basic "rules" to bear in mind that apply to all formats of a resume.

- **Keep the formatting simple**; don't use fancy fonts, graphics, or other attention-grabbing techniques.
- **Use appropriate grammar and spelling**, as defined by the country where the organization you are applying for a job is located. For example, avoid British English if you are applying for a job in the United States or Canada.
- **Proofread your resume**; it is difficult to proofread your own work and you will miss errors, so get someone else to review it.

Again, most of this should be obvious, but I have seen so much of this advice ignored, that I felt I needed to cover it.

Experience Focus

While I have used the generic term "resume" up to this point, what we are really talking about when applying for a DBA position, is a "technical resume" that focuses on your technical skills and experience. When applying for a DBA job, the hiring manager doesn't care if you were on the honor roll in high school, or if you were president of your senior class. The manager is

Chapter 10: Get An Exceptional DBA Job

only interested in your technical skills and experience, so that is where your focus must lie.

In order for your resume to stand out from the crowd, you need to put yourself in the shoes of the hiring manager. You need to ask yourself this: if I were to hire a new DBA, what would I look for in a resume?

First and foremost, as a hiring manager, you would probably be looking for a resume that checked as many boxes as possible in terms of *demonstrated* ability to do the sort of job that you need the candidate to do.

From the job seeker's perspective, that means you should customize your resume for the specific requirements of the job. That way, it will make it much easier for the hiring manager to mentally compare your skills and experience with the skills and experience required by the job. Too many people create a single version of their resume and use it to apply for all of the jobs that interest them. This is a mistake. The closer you can tailor the resume to match the job description, the better off you will be.

In many resumes I have seen, the work experience section is little more than a list of companies, job titles, employment dates, with the briefest of descriptions of what each job entailed. Again, this is one of the biggest mistakes you can make. How can a hiring manager make a decision on a resume with such little information? You need to include a detailed description *what you accomplished* in each job. For example, let's say that you have listed the following work experience on your resume:

- **TechnoBabble Technology**; 2005 to present *SQL Server Database Administrator.*
  Worked as a production DBA managing 25 SQL Servers.

While the above description is accurate and succinct, it is not useful to a hiring manager. This is a more useful example of a work experience description:

- **TechnoBabble Technology**, 2005 to present, *SQL Server Database Administrator.*
  As the lead SQL Server DBA, installed and managed 3 SQL Server 2005 clusters and 22 stand-alone instances, including SQL Server 2000, 2005, and 2008. Performed daily monitoring to ensure an availability of 99.2 percent in the last 4 years. Worked with third-party vendors and in-house developers to optimize the performance of all

Chapter 10: Get An Exceptional DBA Job

database applications, and achieved an average of more than 50% performance boost on 3 mission critical applications. Created and tested disaster recovery plan on annual basis.

In other words, a work experience description needs to include specific facts, emphasizing exactly what you have accomplished in your job that will be directly relevant to the hiring manager.

Of course, this assumes your skill set meets the job description. If the job description and your skill set and experience don't match, the first question you have to ask yourself is if this job is really a job that meets your needs and wants. If it doesn't, then don't bother applying for the job. If the job does sound ideal, but your skill set and experience don't match as ideally as you would like, do the best you can to put a favorable spin on your skills in your resume, while not stretching the truth. Rarely will a hiring manager hire a person that fits a job description exactly. Instead, the hiring manager will be looking for someone that or she feels will be able to do the job to the best of their ability. So if you come up short in a few areas, don't worry, just make your best impression. And the best way to do this is to tailor your resume to match what you think the hiring manager is looking for.

Length and Format

Generally, the more detail you can provide in your resume, the better. I say "generally", because a paper resume has limited space. If you have the room, use it, but if you don't, for example because you have had a large number of jobs, then you will have to include less detail.

Printed technical resumes should generally not exceed two pages in length. Any experience not directly relevant to the job for which you are applying should be removed. Most hiring managers don't have time to wade through lots of unrelated details.

Your goal is to create a two-page targeted resume that gets the interest of a hiring manager (this is kind of like how the director of an action thriller tries to draw in the audience during the first few minutes of the film). Having attracted their attention, you can, at the end of the resume, include a link to an online version of your resume, containing full details of your education, training, skills, experience, articles, books, speaking engagements, community work, peer recommendations and more.

Unlike a standard resume, which should be targeted, an **online resume** is designed to provide a comprehensive review of your career and so can be much longer, and doesn't need to be customized for every job for which you are applying.

The online resume can be located on your own website or blog or, alternatively, on a business-related social networking site like *LinkedIn.com*, the latter being pretty much set up to display this sort of information in a set format.

No matter where you locate your online resume, be sure to include the most important details at the top, as the hiring manager may not take the time to read the entire document. Also, don't include personal details that are unrelated to your job, such as hobbies or special causes in which you are involved. If you have a FaceBook, or other personal social networking pages where you keep in touch with friends, don't include a link to them, although be aware that the hiring manager may find them and check them out anyway.

Tips for Surviving an Interview

Just as a resume is almost always required before getting a new job, so is the interview (sometimes multiple interviews). And just as a resume needs to be thoroughly and carefully prepared, so do you, before you enter the interview room. By this stage, I'm going to assume you've done your basic research and have found out all you possibly can about the role and the organization. You don't want to be asking questions like, "What does your company do?" Don't laugh; it happens.

When you first decide to apply for a job, you probably won't know what style of interview will be eventually conducted, unless you know people at the company you can talk to. In addition, you will have no control over the interview process. Whatever you get subjected to, that will be your fate.

I have been interviewed five different times for DBA jobs. Of these interviews, three of them were "traditional" interviews where I was asked a lot of general questions about my experience, and only a few technical questions. In the other two, I was barraged with a range of often-obscure SQL Server-related technical questions. Now I have a confession to make: I passed the three traditional interviews, and got the jobs, but failed both the technical interviews spectacularly. That's quite a confession, so I had better explain.

Chapter 10: Get An Exceptional DBA Job

In the case of the traditional interviews, I was able to demonstrate that I was properly qualified and experienced enough to perform the job duties. This was all done without answering many specific technical questions. Instead, I was asked about my training, certifications (which indicate at least a passing knowledge of SQL Server), but most of all, my *previous experience* as a DBA. I was able to talk about what I did and how I did it. In a sense, during these interviews, I became my resume, but in the flesh. I was confident in my skills, and myself, and I think that went a long way to getting hired.

So, why did I fail the technical interviews? I was at a stage in my career where I considered myself to be a technically competent and highly capable DBA, so it was not lack of experience or knowledge. In short, first and foremost, it was **lack of preparation**. Having sailed through my previous "traditional" interviews, I had carelessly assumed that other interviews would be the same. I had not asked the right kinds of questions during the phone pre-interviews, and so was unprepared for the sort of interview I was going to face.

My lack of preparation was compounded by the simple fact that I'm not very good at taking tests, of any kind. While I have always "survived", and passed many tests in school, I suffer from "test anxiety". In one of the two technical interviews, there were three DBAs from the organization in the room asking me as difficult questions as they could think of, trying to put me on the spot, which they successfully did. I just wasn't able to think fast enough on my feet to answer many of their questions, although if I had some time, I would have been able to correctly answer them. Ultimately, the pressure of the interview got to me.

So, my golden piece of advice for any DBA facing an interview, especially if you're like me and get test anxiety, is this: gather as much information as you can about the sort of interview you'll be given, and then **be prepared**. Will there be only one interview, or multiple interviews? How many people will be interviewing you, and who are they? What style of interview should you expect?

Once you have this information, you can take the time to become properly prepared to take it on, both psychologically and technically. If it's to be a "conventional" interview, be prepared to answer direct questions that will demonstrate your ability to tackle all of the typical DBA tasks, covered in Chapter 3, that are relevant to the job. You should also have good answers prepared for those "typical" interview questions, such as "What is your

Chapter 10: Get An Exceptional DBA Job

strongest point?" or "What is weakest point?". A search of the Internet may offer some useful advice on how to tackle such questions, though you should avoid "typical answers" as far as possible.

> **NOTE:**
> For information on how to do your best during an interview, conduct an Internet search on "how to do an interview".

If you find out that you will be subjected to a technical-style interview, you will need to prepare thoroughly. In fact, I would prepare for it as if you were studying to take your SQL Server certification tests. Again, a search of the Internet will reveal articles discussing the kinds of technical questions that are often asked during technical interviews of DBAs.

Different companies have wildly different approaches to conducting interviews. Some take the conventional biographical-style interview approach, some use a behavioral approach, some take a technical approach, and some organizations conduct interviews that can best be described as bizarre. In one job I applied for, before I was a DBA, I had everyone in the entire department (about 20 people) come into the room and fire questions at me for about an hour. Surprisingly enough, I actually got that job.

In another non-conventional job interview, I had to make a formal presentation in front of about 30 people, and then answer questions about the presentation from the audience. However, I knew about this one ahead of time and was prepared, and I got that job also.

In the case of the two interviews I failed, I had followed my own advice of not quitting a job before looking for a new one and, ultimately, ended up getting better opportunities by being patient. However, I would ask this of the hiring manager who is partial to the "deep technical" interview: is it more important that a prospective DBA knows every single T-SQL option, or that they are going to be able to get along with the rest of your team? Is it really important that they are able to answer obscure technical questions? Isn't that what Books Online, Kalen Delaney's books, and the Internet are for?

While technical skills are important for a DBA, so are many other skills, and just because a candidate can't answer every obscure question you throw at them doesn't mean they will not be an Exceptional DBA for you. My advice to hiring managers is to focus your technical questions around day-to-day tasks that DBAs need to perform successfully in order to do their job.

While the main purpose of the interview, from the perspective of the hiring organization, is to evaluate you, make sure you take this opportunity to interview the people interviewing you. You want to see if the company meets your needs and wants. In most cases, one of the questions you will be asked in any first interview is if you have any questions, and they will *expect* you to have some! So take advantage of this offer and find out what you need to know, although bear in mind that certain questions, such as "what is the salary?" may not be appropriate for a first interview

Finally, but importantly, despite the pressures and anxiety of the interview process, try to relax and be yourself. Talk with confidence about your experience, but try to avoid coming across as pompous, or as a know-it-all. I talked to a senior DBA at a large company recently, who is the hiring manager, and he told me about a technically qualified candidate he interviewed who was so self-important and pretentious during the interview, that the hiring manager had to keep himself from chuckling because of the spectacle the candidate was making of himself.

What if, after all your hard work and preparation, you fail your interview, and don't get the job? Well, first, maybe you didn't fail the interview; perhaps you did a great job, and the reason you didn't get the job was because there was a lot of competition and the person who got the job just had more relevant experience. If you do feel you underperformed, as I did during my two technical interviews, learn from the experience, work on honing your interview skills, and try again. Be patient, because if you are persistent, and you aspire to be an Exceptional DBA, you will eventually find the job you want.

Chapter 10: Get An Exceptional DBA Job

How to Make a Good First Impression in Your New Job

Congratulations, you found your ideal DBA job and you have been hired! What next? At this point, I suggest you re-read Chapter 8 in this book, *Manage your Brand within your Organization*. In other words, it is very important that you make a great first impression when you start your new job. You should immediately begin thinking about how you will best fit into this position, and the organization, over the long term. Here are some specific tips to get you started on the right foot:

- **Observe and learn**. Take the pulse of the organization and of the people you work with. Find out what they are interested in, what their biggest work issues are, and get a feel for how people interact with one another. The last thing you want to do in a new job is to start telling everyone else how to do their jobs (I have seen this happen). Be patient, take it all in, and once you have a good feel for the group dynamics of your organization, then you will know better how you can fit it.
- **Fitting in does not mean conforming**. Fitting in means finding out not only how you can meet the requirements of your job, but also how your job can meet your needs and wants. Your goal should be to help others get what they want so that you can get what you want.
- **Begin building great relationships with those you work with**. You may have to take the initiative to build these relationships, as some current employees may be a little suspicious of a new employee, and whether or not you can succeed at your new job. This may take time, but will benefit you in the long run as you establish yourself in the organization.
- **Be an Exceptional DBA**. Learn about your job and find out what problems need to be fixed, and identify where you might be able to implement better, more efficient, approaches. This is part of your job, and indicates that you are a proactive DBA.

Once the newness of the job wears off, then it will be your responsibility to keep your job interesting and challenging. No one else is going to do this for you; it is a task you alone must undertake.

Chapter 10: Get An Exceptional DBA Job

Summary: Getting an Exceptional DBA Job is Hard, but the Rewards are High

There are many reasons why you might want to change your job, as this is normal part of every DBA's career. It is important that, as far as possible, you leave your current job on good terms, are able to identify and get a DBA job that comes as close as possible as meeting your wants and needs. This includes learning how to take the job application process in stride, and making the most out of your new job once you have it.

CHAPTER 11: THE EXCEPTIONAL DBA'S CODE OF CONDUCT

Physicians, attorneys, accountants, engineers, realtors, and many other professionals have written guidelines designed to discourage misconduct and illegal activity, and to promote the ethical conduct of their members. In fact, according to the Sarbanes-Oxley act, all public companies in the United States are required to create and follow their own code of conduct.

However, despite the fact that DBAs are essentially protectors of an organization's knowledge, and privy to much confidential information, there is no clearly defined set of rules, values, standards, and guidelines to help govern and guide their behavior.

In this chapter, I define what a code of conduct is, explain how it can be useful to DBAs and the organizations they work for, and consider if and how it could be enforced. Finally, I offer my take on a "Code of Conduct" for the Exceptional DBA. Rather than be prescriptive, my goal is simply to offer advice to DBAs on how they might conduct themselves within the bounds of the professional responsibilities of their job.

What is a Code of Conduct?

Generally speaking, a code of conduct is a set of formal, written rules, policies, standards, guidelines, obligations, behaviors, expectations, and principles that are voluntarily adhered to by a group of people with similar goals, values, and responsibilities. While other definitions exist, this one will serve our purpose well enough, as we seek to define the standards of conduct to which a DBA should adhere while carrying out their professional duties.

Chapter 11: The Exceptional DBA's Code of Conduct

> **NOTE**
> For different perspectives on this topic, you can explore these websites:
> - The Association for Computing Machinery (ACM) at www.acm.org/about/code-of-ethics
> - The Association of Information Technology Professionals (AITP) at www.aitp.org/organization/about/ethics/ethics.jsp

How Can a Code of Conduct be Useful to DBAs?

To many people, a "Code of Conduct" means one thing: more rules. Most DBAs, myself included, would consider themselves mature enough to make their own decisions and choices, and are naturally resistant to the idea of someone telling them what to do and how to do it.

If this is the case, then why have I written this chapter? Well, first, my intent is not to offer a set of rules that have to be followed but, instead, a set of guidelines that can be useful for DBAs who want to fully understand and appreciate the nature and scope of their duties and responsibilities. In other words, it is intended to be educational.

At a fundamental level, most DBAs believe they understand what it means to behave "ethically". In my experience, instances of willful negligence, or blatantly unethical behavior, are relatively scarce in our profession. However, there are many "grey" areas where a DBA, especially a less-experienced DBA, can find themselves unsure of where their responsibilities end, and how exactly they should respond to a potentially compromising situation.

For example if, as a DBA, you identify criminal behavior within your organization, what do you do? Hopefully, your answer would be that you'd report it. However, is that the end of your responsibilities? What if the company you work for does not respond appropriately? What further action should you take, if any?

It's a sad fact that many organizations don't fully understand and appreciate the true role of a DBA. In their attempts to save money, they sometimes cut corners that can directly affect the integrity of their data, and so unwittingly place the guardians of their data in a difficult dilemma. If you find yourself in this situation then, hopefully, this code of conduct may help convince your organization of the importance of the role of the DBA, and the need to employ experienced DBAs to safeguard their business data. For example, if you are having difficulty convincing your manager to adhere to government regulation that affects the data you manage, then referring the manager to this Code of Conduct might be useful.

Perhaps above all else, the "Exceptional DBA's Code of Conduct" can be a source of pride to all of us who choose to adhere to it, and give us more confidence that we are doing the best we can at our jobs.

How Should a Code of Conduct be Implemented and Enforced?

Whenever the topic of a "code of conduct" is discussed, one of the first questions to be asked is: how can it be enforced? After all, if the code is not enforced in any way then, it is argued, who is it benefiting? There is no straightforward answer to the question of how to enforce such a code, or even if it should be enforced, rather than be voluntary.

One suggestion is that the code be enforced by an independent, professional organization, such as the ACM, AITP, or PASS. Anyone who fails to follow the established code of conduct could have their membership of the organization revoked. On the assumption that most businesses would regard membership of the organization a key requirement in their hiring process, then it could, in theory, prove an effective deterrent to malpractice.

Another suggestion is that organizations that offer DBA certifications, such as Microsoft, should enforce some code of conduct. Again, any DBA who fails to follow the established code could have their certification rescinded. Obviously, this would only be an effective measure for organizations that require certification as part of their terms of employment. On the other hand, if Microsoft were to attempt this, what about the Oracle and MySQL DBAs? Would they need a separate code that is tied to their certifications?

Another option is to have a DBA Code of Conduct enforced on a per-organization basis. After all, many organizations already require their employers to abide by a "code of conduct," often in the form of an employee handbook. Such a code could be expanded to incorporate conduct specific to DBAs. On the other hand, if a company creates a separate code of conduct for

Chapter 11: The Exceptional DBA's Code of Conduct

DBAs, wouldn't it also have to create different codes of conduct for other job titles? Again, this is not a great solution.

In light of the numerous complications of implementing and enforcing a DBA's Code of Conduct, I suggest that following such a code, or not, is the personal choice of the individual DBA. As I noted earlier, I regard such as code as being primarily educational in nature, with the rewards for following it being a successful, rewarding, long-term, and satisfying career as a DBA. For those who choose not to follow it, well, who knows how their career will turn out? They might get lucky and survive over the long haul, but I doubt if they will ever fall into the Exceptional DBA category.

The Exceptional DBA's Code of Conduct

This section contains my suggestions for the core items that should comprise "The Exceptional DBA's Code of Conduct". My focus is on providing general guidelines that will help any DBA become more successful in their career.

I won't be so presumptuous as to imply that these guidelines are ideal or exhaustive, but they should hopefully get you thinking and be a useful guide to you in your role as a DBA.

Protection and Disclosure of Data

1. DBAs shall never intentionally do anything that contributes to the corruption or loss of an organization's data. While this should be a no-brainer, I am including the obvious, just to cover all the bases.

2. Above all else, the DBA is the guardian, or protector, of an organization's data. The responsibilities of the DBA in this regard include but are not limited to:

    - Preventing data corruption (from applications, hardware, and people).
    - Provide high data availability, as defined by the organization's policy.
    - Develop, and regularly test, a disaster recovery plan to minimize unexpected downtime, as defined by the organization's policy.

Chapter 11: The Exceptional DBA's Code of Conduct

3. DBAs shall take all reasonable precautions to ensure that changes to a production server have no detrimental consequences. All proposed changes should be thoroughly tested on a test server prior to deployment to production.
4.
5. DBAs shall proactively take all the necessary steps to ensure that data can only be accessed by authorized users. This may include, but is not limited to: SQL Server security, Windows Authentication security, encryption, SQL injection attack prevention, auditing, or other such security policies, as defined by their organization.

6. DBAs generally have full access to all the data in a database. This presents two important points:

    - DBAs shall only view data in a database if they need to access it to perform their job duties. For example, a DBA may need to access data to optimize a query or create a report. But if the DBA doesn't need to access and view data for job-related tasks, then DBAs shall not snoop through the data for the sake of viewing it.
    - If, during the course of their required job duties, DBAs do view confidential data, DBAs shall not share any sensitive or confidential information with any unauthorized users.

7. DBAs shall provide full cooperation with both inside and outside audits, providing truthful and factual information.
8.
9. If the DBA learns that contractors, co-workers, or managers are making poor choices that could negatively affect the integrity or security of the organization's data, then the DBA should notify the appropriate persons within their organization.
10.
11. If a DBA discovers misuse of an organization's data, then the DBA should report this behavior to the appropriate persons within their organization.

12. The DBA should maintain proper and complete documentation for all servers and processes for which he or she is responsible. The documentation should be of a form and standard that will allow a

Chapter 11: The Exceptional DBA's Code of Conduct

qualified peer to undertake the task, in the DBA's absence. The DBA should never protect (hide) information from their organization that would prevent another person from easily taking over his or her position, should the need arise.

DBAs and the Law

1. Often, the data under the care of a DBA is subject to laws and regulations of one or more governing bodies. The DBA shall become familiar with these laws and regulations, and adhere to them.

2. The DBA shall enforce all software licensing agreement with vendors, and notify the proper people in the organization if any breech is discovered.

3. If the DBA becomes aware of illegal activity within their organization, the DBA shall notify the proper people in their organization, or the appropriate law enforcement agency.

Dealing With Third-Parties

1. DBAs shall not accept gifts or favors from vendors if the purpose of the gift or favor is to influence, or to reward, the DBA's choice of purchasing goods and services from the vendor. More specifically:

    - The DBA shall proactively learn their organization's policies about gifts, so they know what they can or cannot accept. For example, company policy might allow a vendor to take a DBA to dinner, or to receive a free gift at a conference or a user's group meeting. On the other hand, an organization's policy might limit the amount of the gift to a maximum value, such as $50.00.
    - The acceptance of a gift, even if allowed by the organization, should not influence the behavior of the DBA in regards to potential purchase of the vendor's products and services.
    - Whenever a DBA purchases, or influences the purchase of goods or services, the DBA should only purchase those good or services because they are the ones that best meet the needs of the organization.

Chapter 11: The Exceptional DBA's Code of Conduct

General Conduct

- The DBA shall conduct himself, or herself, professionally in all relationships with the people they deal with on a daily basis, including managers, co-workers, vendors, and their "internal customers." Favoritism and discrimination of any sort is to be avoided.

- If a DBA makes a mistake, and all DBAs make a mistake at one time or another, the mistake should be fixed as soon as is practical, and the DBA should inform everyone who might be negatively affected by the mistake as soon as possible. In addition:

- Mistakes should never be covered up.

- DBAs should take full responsibility for all their decisions.

- If a DBA has management responsibilities, the DBA should mentor those who need help accomplishing their objectives, and allow those with experience and enthusiasm to succeed and flourish within the environment he or she provides for them.

- The DBA will do their job to the best of his or her ability, developing and implementing best practices as appropriate, to help ensure the smooth and successful operations of the organization's databases.

- IT technology changes quickly. It is the responsibility of the DBA to proactively keep up on all technical areas that directly affect their job.

- If the DBA has agreed to a SLA (Service Level Agreement) for the servers under their care, then they will abide by those agreements. If they are not technically able to abide by the agreed upon SLA (for whatever reason), the DBA needs to contact the SLA owner and work out how to resolve the problem.

- Occasionally, the DBA may find that there is no established policy with regard to a particular aspect of their duties. For example, perhaps an organization doesn't have a policy that defines the desired level of uptime, or that defines who can access what data. In areas where policies should be established (to ensure the protection and integrity of the organization's data), but are not established, the DBA shall proactively identify the areas of need, make recommendations, and present them to the organization's management so they can make appropriate decisions.

It is impossible to provide advice to guide a DBA through every aspect of their duties and responsibilities as a DBA, and there are many "grey areas". What does the DBA do when they notify the appropriate persons of an important issue that could negatively impact the organization's data, and no action is taken to rectify the issue? Where do a DBA's responsibilities end with regard to uncovering illegal activity within an organization? What does a DBA do when a cost-cutting measure means they feel they can't fully adhere to their own code of conduct? These are all difficult questions for any employee, not just a DBA.

If you, as a DBA, feel "pressured" to do something you are uncomfortable doing, then the best advice I can give is to talk to people. In most cases, the first step is to tell your manager, co-worker, project manager, or whoever is causing the problem, that you feel uncomfortable with their request, action or inaction, and explain why. If they don't want to listen, your next option is to escalate the issue to their manager. You may, or may not, receive management support for your case. If not, then you have to decide to "give in", or to find another job.

The key thing is that the DBA needs to keep cool and not take any rash action. Before making an important decision that could potentially hurt your career, talk over the issue with people you trust in order to get their feedback and input. Only take action once you have clearly and thoughtfully considered the consequences of your choices. This might mean keeping quiet and not making trouble, escalating the issue to higher levels of management, reporting a crime to an enforcement agency, or finding a new job.

Chapter 11: The Exceptional DBA's Code of Conduct

Summary: Exceptional DBAs are defined by their Actions

My goal in suggesting an "Exceptional DBA's Code of Conduct" is to provide advice and guidance for those DBAs wanting to learn more about what it takes to become an Exceptional DBA. Is the code complete or perfect? Of course not. Consider it a working, educational document; it is certainly not intended to be an absolute set of rules that every DBA must always follow.

My hope is that it serves as a useful guide to the DBAs looking to navigate the "grey areas" and as a foundation for all those entering the profession with ambitions to become Exceptional DBAs.

Chapter 12: Best Practices for Becoming an Exceptional DBA

We have covered a lot of ground in the past eleven chapters. In this final chapter, I want to summarize the keys traits, skills and habits that I believe will help you become an Exceptional DBA. In keeping with SQL Server tradition, I have tried to express them in the form of "best practices" recommendations for becoming an Exceptional DBA, which (hopefully) are straightforward and easy to follow.

In addition, I'd like to use this chapter as a "call for action." As with any book, information is worthless unless you actually apply it. Becoming an Exceptional DBA is an achievable task; you just have to make the decision to become one.

Best Practices

In the following sections, I provide a set of best practice recommendations for becoming an Exceptional DBA. However, please don't assume that they form an A-to-Z path to reaching that goal. You don't need to have every single skill or trait that I cover here in order to become an Exceptional DBA. You need to review each best practice and evaluate its relevance to you, both as a person and as a DBA. Some of the best practices will seem obvious to you, and most likely will be easy for you to achieve. Other recommendations may be a poor fit for you, or very difficult to achieve. There are many different paths to becoming an Exceptional DBA. You just have to pick the path that works best for you, and follow it.

Chapter 12: Best Practices for Becoming an Exceptional DBA

Character Traits

Exceptional DBAs are not defined by how much they know about SQL Server, but by their actions. More specifically, the Exceptional DBA:

Enjoys Technology

Enjoys Challenge

Enjoys Problem Solving

Embraces Change

Enjoys Learning

Accepts Responsibility

Maintains Professionalism

Is Trustworthy

Is Dependable

Is Hard-Working

Can Work Well Independently or in a Team

Manages Time Well

Can Communicate Effectively, Both Orally and Verbally

Listens Well

Is Realistic

Is Flexible

Is Patient

Is Persistent

Is Enthusiastic

Thinks Before Acting

Is Mature

Is Self-Confident

Chapter 12: Best Practices for Becoming an Exceptional DBA

- Exceptional DBAs not only enjoy learning, they are lifelong learners. They take every available opportunity to maintain and broaden their skill sets.

- Exceptional DBAs share their knowledge freely, with other people in their organization, with the SQL Server community at large and, when possible, by mentoring new DBAs.

- Exceptional DBAs become DBAs because they enjoy their work. It is challenging, changing, and fast-paced. In most cases, they are DBAs not just because they can earn a good living at it, but because they enjoy what they do.

Hard Skills

- DBAs are tasked with protecting an organization's data. The Exceptional DBA fully understands this responsibility and takes it very seriously.

- The Exceptional DBA is not content to master just the fundamentals of SQL Server. He or she also specializes in one or more areas, and comes to know them "inside and out." These specialist areas can include System Administration, Database Design, Development, High Availability, Business Intelligence, Report Writing, among others.

- Exceptional DBAs know that in order to fully understand and troubleshoot SQL Server, they must have a good understanding of computer hardware, operating systems, networking, and best practices.

- Exceptional DBAs must master the tools of the trade. This includes both the tools provided with SQL Server, and any third-party tools they can use to boost their productivity and help ensure the integrity of the data they protect.

- While not a requirement, most Exceptional DBAs have a four-year degree, which may or may not be in information technology. Completing a university degree, no matter the subject, is a strong

Chapter 12: Best Practices for Becoming an Exceptional DBA

indicator that an individual is able to learn and survive in a challenging environment.

- Although not a requirement, many Exceptional DBAs will have one or more professional certifications. Not only does this help the DBA gain a wider knowledge of SQL Server, it also helps to demonstrate to others how seriously they are committed to their career.

- It takes time to become an Exceptional DBA. Actual production experience is the best teacher of all, and is one of the most important things employers or customers look for when hiring a DBA.

- Many DBAs have the opportunity to lead projects. The Exceptional DBA has good project management skills and knows how to lead a team to project success.

- Whether we like it or not, DBAs are becoming more and more involved with legal issues. The Exceptional DBAs ensure that they understand their legal responsibilities.

Soft Skills

- Exceptional DBAs work with many different people, in many different departments of their organization, from clerks all the way to CEOs. They know how to work well with others, even those they may not personally like.

- Many DBA tasks are done alone, while others are performed as part of a team. The Exceptional DBA is equally at home in either situation.

- DBAs often have to write reports, proposals and documentation. In addition, they may have to chair meetings, make presentations, or train others. The Exceptional DBA has excellent writing and verbal communication skills.

- As a DBA, you must communicate effectively. Communication does not just mean talking to your team members and boss. It includes writing effective e-mails, status reports, check lists, documentation, presentations and database diagrams. Even that is no longer enough; you must ensure that the company, as a whole, understands what you are doing and how your work contributes to the business.

- As an important adjunct to having good writing and verbal communication skills, Exceptional DBAs are also good listeners. Often, the person requesting the services of the DBA really doesn't know how to formulate their request properly and accurately. The Exceptional DBA listens carefully and asks the right questions in order to find out what the user really needs.

- Exceptional DBAs are often leaders. They may be a leader in the formal role of a manager, or they may be a leader in terms of initiating new ideas and actions within an organization.

- Most DBAs are overworked and underappreciated. In order to keep up with the many tasks they need to perform, the Exceptional DBA knows how to manage time well.

- Exceptional DBAs understand that the world, their organization, and their job is not perfect. They have realistic expectations and roll with the punches when necessary. On the other hand, the Exceptional DBA knows when to take a strong stand, and how to defend his or her position robustly, but appropriately.

Branding

Exceptional DBAs know that in order to accomplish their goals, they need the help of others. They take control of their own personal branding within their organization so that people fully understand what they are about, and where they are coming from. Some of the ways they accomplish this include:

- Focusing on business goals
- Being a leader and taking the initiative
- Volunteering for hard or undesirable tasks
- Having a get it done attitude
- Not blaming others
- Accepting responsibility

Chapter 12: Best Practices for Becoming an Exceptional DBA

- Not abusing their power
- Helping others be successful
- By not playing office politics
- Understanding the "geek factor" and how it affects others
- Adopting good e-mail etiquette
- Fully participating in meetings
- Making good presentations
- Having International/Cultural Sensitivity
- Using technology and tools to become more productive

Exceptional DBAs also realize the importance of managing their online brand and takes steps to ensure that their online branding is as positive as possible. Some of the ways they do this include:

- Taking the time to evaluate their current online presence to determine what kind of image they have.
- Taking steps to get negative information removed from the web, if possible.
- Taking the initiative to improve and expand their online profile, where they can, by supplying content that positively displays their skills, experience, and professionalism.

Career Management

- Exceptional DBAs take control of their careers, rather than let their career control them.

- Exceptional DBAs decide what they want from their career, and take actions to make it happen.

- Exceptional DBAs know how to set realistic, short-term goals in order to reach major milestones in their career plan.

- Exceptional DBAs know that if they don't follow through with their goals, then nobody else will do it for them. They are self-motivated and ready for action.

Chapter 12: Best Practices for Becoming an Exceptional DBA

- Exceptional DBAs realize that career plans and goals can change, and regularly reevaluate and revise their career path.

Summary: The GOYA Principle

When I was at university, I took a class in management, taught by the Dean of the business department. The Dean showed us a movie, mysteriously titled GOYA. It was one of those cheaply made management-training films that many of you have probably seen at some time or another. However, unlike most of the training films I have seen, this one has stuck with me for many years.

You might be familiar with a famous Spanish painter by the name of Goya, and most of the audience assumed that the movie was going to draw some parallels between good management practices and Goya's paintings or painting techniques. As the film proceeded, the artist Goya was never mentioned. Instead, we were confronted with many badly-acted scenes showing lazy workers going about their work, but mainly accomplishing nothing. This got a little boring very quickly and was not very inspiring.

At the end of the film, it cut to a screen with the letters GOYA displayed in large type. Some of the audience members were shooting each other puzzled looks, when the film suddenly cut to very final screen that said, "Get Off Your Ass!"

This was a surprise ending to the film, but it made an important point that I want to share with you. The point is that if you want to be an Exceptional DBA, you can't wait until it happens to you, because it won't. If you want to be an Exceptional DBA, you must get off your ass and make it happen. Nobody is going to help you. There is no magic pixie dust.

More specifically, you need to:

- Decide what you want out of your career as a DBA
- Develop specific goals that describe how you intend to attain your career plans
- Take action today, no matter how small, to accomplish your goals
- Revaluate and revise your goals as necessary
- Don't give up

Chapter 12: Best Practices for Becoming an Exceptional DBA

Don't wait. Start right now. After finishing this book, immediately take some small step to get yourself going. It might be making a forum post, reading an article or blog on SQL Server, reading a chapter of a SQL Server book that has been collecting dust on a shelf, writing down your career plans, or signing up to take a class. Whatever action you decide to take, do it now, today, before you lose your motivation. I can tell you from personal experience, if you want to accomplish a major life goal, the only way to attain it is through hard work and perseverance.

.NET and SQL Server Tools
from Red Gate Software

Pricing and information about Red Gate tools are correct at the time of going to print. For the latest information and pricing on all Red Gate's tools, visit www.red-gate.com

redgate®

ingeniously simple tools

ANTS Memory Profiler $495
Find memory leaks and optimize memory usage

- Find memory leaks within minutes
- Jump straight to the heart of the problem with intelligent summary information, filtering options and visualizations
- Optimize the memory usage of your C# and VB.NET code

> "Freaking sweet! We have a known memory leak that took me about four hours to find using our current tool, so I fired up ANTS Memory Profiler and went at it like I didn't know the leak existed. Not only did I come to the conclusion much faster, but I found another one!"
> **Aaron Smith** IT Manager, R.C. Systems Inc.

ANTS Performance Profiler from $395
Profile your .NET code and boost the performance of your application

- Identify performance bottlenecks within minutes
- Drill down to slow lines of code thanks to line-level code timings
- Boost the performance of your .NET code
- Get the most complete picture of your application's performance with integrated SQL and File I/O profiling

> "Thanks to ANTS Performance Profiler, we were able to discover a performance hit in our serialization of XML that was fixed for a 10x performance increase."
> **Garret Spargo** Product Manager, AFHCAN

> "ANTS Performance Profiler took us straight to the specific areas of our code which were the cause of our performance issues."
> **Terry Phillips** Sr Developer, Harley-Davidson Dealer Systems

Visit **www.red-gate.com** for a 14-day, free trial

.NET Reflector ®   From $35
Browse, compile, analyze and decompile .NET code

- View, navigate and search through the class hierarchies of .NET assemblies, even if you don't have access to the source code for them
- Decompile and analyze .NET assemblies in C#, Visual Basic and IL
- Step into decompiled assemblies whilst debugging in Visual Studio, with all the debugging techniques you would use on your own code

> "One of the most useful, practical debugging tools that I have ever worked with in .NET! It provides complete browsing and debugging features for .NET assemblies, and has clean integration with Visual Studio."
> **Tom Baker** Consultant Software Engineer, EMC Corporation

SmartAssembly ®   from $795
.NET obfuscator and automated error reporting

- Obfuscate your .NET code and protect your IP
- Let your end-users report errors in your software with one click
- Receive a comprehensive report containing a stack trace and values of all the local variables
- Identify the most recurrent bugs and prioritize fixing those first
- Gather feature usage data to understand how your software is being used and make better product development decisions

> "I've deployed Automated Error Reporting now for one release and I'm already seeing the benefits. I can fix bugs which might never have got my attention before. I really like it a lot!"
> Stefal Koell MVP

Visit **www.red-gate.com** for a 14-day, free trial

SQL Compare® Pro $595
Compare and synchronize SQL Server database schemas

- ↗ Eliminate mistakes migrating database changes from dev, to test, to production
- ↗ Speed up the deployment of new databse schema updates
- ↗ Find and fix errors caused by differences between databases
- ↗ Compare and synchronize within SSMS

> "Just purchased SQL Compare. With the productivity I'll get out of this tool, it's like buying time."
> **Robert Sondles** Blueberry Island Media Ltd

SQL Data Compare Pro $595
Compares and synchronizes SQL Server database contents

- ↗ Save time by automatically comparing and synchronizing your data
- ↗ Copy lookup data from development databases to staging or production
- ↗ Quickly fix problems by restoring damaged or missing data to a single row
- ↗ Compare and synchronize data within SSMS

> "We use SQL Data Compare daily and it has become an indispensable part of delivering our service to our customers. It has also streamlined our daily update process and cut back literally a good solid hour per day."
> **George Pantela** GPAnalysis.com

Visit **www.red-gate.com** for a 14-day, free trial

SQL Prompt Pro $295
Write, edit, and explore SQL effortlessly

- Write SQL smoothly, with code-completion and SQL snippets
- Reformat SQL to a preferred style
- Keep databases tidy by finding invalid objects automatically
- Save time and effort with script summaries, smart object renaming and more

> "SQL Prompt is hands-down one of the coolest applications I've used. Makes querying/developing so much easier and faster."
> Jorge Segarra University Community Hospital

SQL Source Control $295
Connect your existing source control system to SQL Server

- Bring all the benefits of source control to your database
- Source control schemas and data within SSMS, not with offline scripts
- Connect your databases to TFS, SVN, SourceGear Vault, Vault Pro, Mercurial, Perforce, Git, Bazaar, and any source control system with a capable command line
- Work with shared development databases, or individual copies
- Track changes to follow who changed what, when, and why
- Keep teams in sync with easy access to the latest database version
- View database development history for easy retrieval of specific versions

> "After using SQL Source Control for several months, I wondered how I got by before. Highly recommended, it has paid for itself several times over"
> Ben Ashley Fast Floor

Visit **www.red-gate.com** for a 28-day, free trial

SQL Backup Pro $795

Compress, encrypt, and strengthen SQL Server backups

- Compress SQL Server database backups by up to 95% for faster, smaller backups
- Protect your data with up to 256-bit AES encryption
- Strengthen your backups with network resilience to enable a fault-tolerant transfer of backups across flaky networks
- Control your backup activities through an intuitive interface, with powerful job management and an interactive timeline

> "SQL Backup is an amazing tool that lets us manage and monitor our backups in real time. Red Gate's SQL tools have saved us so much time and work that I am afraid my director will decide that we don't need a DBA anymore!"
>
> **Mike Poole** Database Administrator, Human Kinetics

Visit **www.red-gate.com** for a 14-day, free trial

SQL Monitor

SQL Server performance monitoring and alerting

- Intuitive overviews at global, cluster, machine, SQL Server, and database levels for up-to-the-minute performance data
- Use SQL Monitor's web UI to keep an eye on server performance in real time on desktop machines and mobile devices
- Intelligent SQL Server alerts via email and an alert inbox in the UI, so you know about problems first
- Comprehensive historical data, so you can go back in time to identify the source of a problem
- Generate reports via the UI or with Red Gate's free SSRS Reporting Pack
- View the top 10 expensive queries for an instance or database based on CPU usage, duration and reads and writes
- PagerDuty integration for phone and SMS alerting
- Fast, simple installation and administration

> "Being web based, SQL Monitor is readily available to you, wherever you may be on your network. You can check on your servers from almost any location, via most mobile devices that support a web browser."
>
> **Jonathan Allen** Senior DBA, Careers South West Ltd

SQL Virtual Restore $495
Rapidly mount live, fully functional databases direct from backups

- ↗ Virtually restoring a backup requires significantly less time and space than a regular physical restore
- ↗ Databases mounted with SQL Virtual Restore are fully functional and support both read/write operations
- ↗ SQL Virtual Restore is ACID compliant and gives you access to full, transactionally consistent data, with all objects visible and available
- ↗ Use SQL Virtual Restore to recover objects, verify your backups with DBCC CHECKDB, create a storage-efficient copy of your production database, and more.

> "We find occasions where someone has deleted data accidentally or dropped an index etc., and with SQL Virtual Restore we can mount last night's backup quickly and easily to get access to the data or the original schema. It even works with all our backups being encrypted. This takes any extra load off our production server. SQL Virtual Restore is a great product."
> **Brent McCraken** Senior Database Administrator/Architect, Kiwibank Limited

SQL Storage Compress $1,595
Silent data compression to optimize SQL Server storage

- ↗ Reduce the storage footprint of live SQL Server databases by up to 90% to save on space and hardware costs
- ↗ Databases compressed with SQL Storage Compress are fully functional
- ↗ Prevent unauthorized access to your live databases with 256-bit AES encryption
- ↗ Integrates seamlessly with SQL Server and does not require any configuration changes

Visit **www.red-gate.com** for a 14-day, free trial

SQL Toolbelt $1,995

The essential SQL Server tools for database professionals

You can buy our acclaimed SQL Server tools individually or bundled. Our most popular deal is the SQL Toolbelt: fourteen of our SQL Server tools in a single installer, with **a combined value of $5,930 but an actual price of $1,995**, a saving of 66%.

Fully compatible with SQL Server 2000, 2005, and 2008.

SQL Toolbelt contains:

- **SQL Compare Pro**
- **SQL Data Compare Pro**
- **SQL Source Control**
- **SQL Backup Pro**
- **SQL Monitor**
- **SQL Prompt Pro**
- **SQL Data Generator**

- **SQL Doc**
- **SQL Dependency Tracker**
- **SQL Packager**
- **SQL Multi Script Unlimited**
- **SQL Search**
- **SQL Comparison SDK**
- **SQL Object Level Recovery Native**

"The SQL Toolbelt provides tools that database developers, as well as DBAs, should not live without."
William Van Orden Senior Database Developer, Lockheed Martin

Visit **www.red-gate.com** for a 14-day, free trial

Performance Tuning with SQL Server Dynamic Management Views

Louis Davidson and Tim Ford

This is the book that will de-mystify the process of using Dynamic Management Views to collect the information you need to troubleshoot SQL Server problems. It will highlight the core techniques and "patterns" that you need to master, and will provide a core set of scripts that you can use and adapt for your own requirements.

ISBN: 978-1-906434-47-2
Published: October 2010

Defensive Database Programming

Alex Kuznetsov

Inside this book, you will find dozens of practical, defensive programming techniques that will improve the quality of your T-SQL code and increase its resilience and robustness.

ISBN: 978-1-906434-49-6
Published: June 2010

Brad's Sure Guide to SQL Server Maintenance Plans

Brad McGehee

Brad's Sure Guide to Maintenance Plans shows you how to use the Maintenance Plan Wizard and Designer to configure and schedule eleven core database maintenance tasks, ranging from integrity checks, to database backups, to index reorganizations and rebuilds.

ISBN: 78-1-906434-34-2
Published: December 2009

The Red Gate Guide to SQL Server Team-based Development

Phil Factor, Grant Fritchey, Alex Kuznetsov, and Mladen Prajdić

This book shows how to use of mixture of home-grown scripts, native SQL Server tools, and tools from the Red Gate SQL Toolbelt, to successfully develop database applications in a team environment, and make database development as similar as possible to "normal" development.

ISBN: 978-1-906434-59-5
Published: November 2010